WHITE CLIFFS MEDIA

Performance in World Music Series

Lawrence Aynesmith, Series Editor

D1501473

MANDIANI
DRUM and DANCE

Djimbe

Performance

and Black

Aesthetics

from Africa

to the

New World

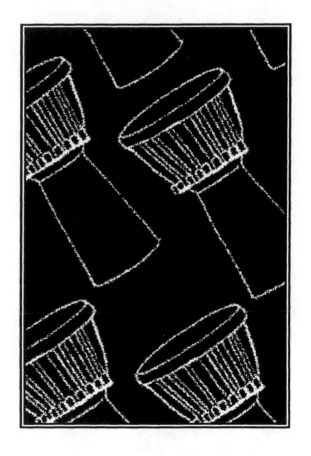

Mark Sunkett

White Cliffs Media, Inc.
Tempe, Arizona

White Cliffs Media
P.O. Box 89
Gilsum, NH 03448

Printed on acid-free paper in the USA

Library of Congress Cataloging in Publication Data

   Sunkett, Mark, 1949-
Mandiani Drum and Dance: Djimbe Performance and Black Aesthetics
from Africa to the New World / Mark Sunkett
     p.   cm.   — (Performance in world music series; no. 9)
     Includes bibliographical references and index.
     ISBN 0-941677-78-8 (cloth)
     ISBN 0-941677-76-1 (pbk.)
     ISBN 0-941677-79-6 (spiral bound)
     ISBN 0-941677-77-X (study audio cassette)
     ISBN 0-9041677-83-4 (study CD)
     ISBN 0-941677-80-X (instructional video)
     ISBN 0-941677-81-8 (performance audio cassette)
     ISBN 0-941677-82-6 (performance audio CD)
     1. Mandingo (African people) — Music — History and criticism.
     2. Folk dance music—Africa, West—History and Criticism.
     3. Musical meter and rhythm. 4. Folk dancing, Mandingo—Africa,
     West. 5. Folk dance music—United States—History and criticism.
     6. Aesthetics, comparative. I. Title. II. Series
     ML 3760.S84 1993
     786.9'0899634 — dc20   93-37626
                                                        CIP
                                                        MN

Contents

List of Figures
Chapter Two

Acknowledgments

A project of this magnitude requires the cooperation of many individuals. The informants who served as contributors to this project have offered their perceptions in a concise and thoughtful way. For each of them, African music and dance are principal forces in their lives. This list of informants and other contributors can't possibly recognize all of the many individual students, ensemble members, and audience participants who contributed to this study. Facilities such as Leslie's Dance and Skate in New York and other locations around the country provided opportunities to view dance and drum classes which were basic to an understanding of African-American aesthetic characteristics and preferences. I want to especially thank both past and present members of the Kawambé Drum and Dance Ensemble of Phoenix, Arizona, for their inspiration and support in preparing this book. The current membership includes Lendo Abdur-Rahman, Adébiyi Banjoko, Melvin Bridges, Consuelo V. Davis, Debbie Glasper, Mariama Thiam, and Carol Simmons. I would also like to thank the University Committee on African and African-American Studies and The College of Fine Arts at Arizona State University for providing grants and funding support.

My sincerest gratitude must be expressed to the drummers and dancers who offered invaluable information leading to my understanding of Mandiani in Africa and the United States. This expression of thanks should be shared with Madjiguene, Vore, Daour and the entire Seck family in Bargny, Sénégal, my home away from home. My appreciation extends to all those informants listed in the Appendix of this book, plus all others unnamed who have contributed to this effort.

I would like to thank Dr. Robert Lord, Dr. Arthur Tuden, and Dr. Bell Yung for their guidance and support. Special recognition must be given to Dr. Nathan Davis and Professor J.H. Kwabena Nketia for their guidance through courses in critical thinking, field research, African, and African-American studies during my studies at the University of Pittsburgh.

Little of this could have taken place without the immeasurable assistance, support, love, and understanding of my wife, Phyllis, and to her, I will be eternally grateful.

Mark Sunkett

Chapter One

Introduction

Mande performance traditions are among the most vibrant found in the African-American community today. This music and dance, indigenous to the countries of Sénégal, Mali and Guinea, spread throughout native societies touched by the Mali Empire between 1200 and 1400 A.D. One of these Mande music and dance traditions is widely known in the African-American community as Mandiani.

The vitality, sheer energy, and athletic display generated in the performance of Mande music and dance was introduced in the United States during the first performances of Guinean and Sénégalese national ballet companies during the late 1950s and 60s. Since then, Mandiani has remained a dominant expression of African culture for African-Americans and is quickly captivating a broad and diverse global community.

Literature, art, theater, and music have all undergone examination for insights into the creative forces, ideas, inspirations, and values which initiate their creation. The music and dance of African-Americans in both recreational and religious settings has become the focus of many contemporary researchers in search of aesthetic explanations. Few of these researchers are pursuing these art forms and subsequent topics with a comprehensive aesthetic approach. This is one of the goals of this study. By examining Mandiani music and dance as it is learned and performed in both Mande and African-American ensembles today, we will encounter a wide range of aesthetic and social issues. The arts, particularly those of music and dance, are an expression of cultural identity and the manifestation of a cultural aesthetic. Music and dance activities provide a physical, observable presentation of aesthetic principles at work within a community. They serve to demonstrate self-recognition and definition.

My primary sources for information from Africa were interviews with musicians and dancers of the Mande cultures who live in the United States or tour with national performance companies from the Mande regions. Observations and interviews with members of the Mande communities and professional performers also took place while visiting Sénégal in the summers of 1987, 1989, 1992 and early 1994.

The concept of a "professional performer" is quite different in most African countries from that of the western art community. When forming professional touring companies in Africa, performers generally are chosen for their talents in the music and dance of their own ethnic group. These individuals typically do not receive training in music and dance at formal institutions prior to joining national companies. As members of the performing company they learn the repertoire of each ethnic group represented in the ensemble. Cultural representations of music and dance within these ensembles are designed expressly for the concert stage.

Methodologies

The methodologies used in this study include participation, observation, and interviews with prominent figures in the African and African-American drum and dance community. Informants are listed in an appendix and their quotes are indented from the main body of the text. Dance classes were visited in Phoenix, Tucson, Los Angeles, Philadelphia, New York City, Washington, D. C. and Atlanta. Classes observed in Africa which were attended by African-Americans and other individuals from a variety of ethnic backgrounds were held in Dakar, Kaolack, and Casamance, Sénégal. We examined aesthetic views of African-Americans involved with Mandiani, including their preferences for instruments, sonic levels, rhythms and rhythmic complexities, and structures in the drum ensemble. In dance we explored kinetic preferences, movement styles, activity levels, body extension, mental and physical states. Physical and psychological gratification among both drummers and dancers was addressed, along with aspects of costuming and accessories.

In this text every attempt is made to address individuals or groups without gender reference unless it is relevant to the discussion. The terms African-American or European-American are used when referring to people or their ideas. References to Black Americans or Blacks appear when used as part of a direct quote, or if significant in the historical context of the passage.

Toward Understanding Aesthetics

Establishing a basic framework for considering aesthetics will provide a general understanding of the approach I take in this writing. In a collection of short essays written in 1928, philosopher Irwin Edman said that lovers of the arts find music, poetry, painting, and the novel as narcotic as they are delightful, and an escape from the pressures and requirements placed upon them by their health, finances, or affections.[1] As a philosopher steeped in traditional concepts of high art, Edman attempted to acknowledge all of the senses but suggested a priority ranking. Sound, sight, touch, and physiological perceptions each contribute to our aesthetic concepts. Edman also sought to include intellect and emotion in his explanation of aesthetics:

> The other senses, too, have their possible aesthetic exploitation, but touch, taste, and smell are not as finely manipulated, not as easily incorporated in objects or detached from practical biological interests as sight and sound.[2]
>
> Aesthetic interest is itself detachment. . . . Color, . . . is the painter's special material. Differences in rhythm and tone, negligible in practical communication, become for the musician the source of all his art, for the music lover the source of all his pleasure. . . . The ear of a listener is the ear of one to whom sounds have associations and of one who has listened to words for their meaning as well as for their tintinnabulation.[3]

Another view of aesthetic thought, presented by Alan P. Merriam in *The Anthropology of Music* is,"The aesthetic implies an attitude which includes values held . . ."[4] These attitudes and values can only be developed by the culture creating what is to be evaluated. At the core of this statement lies the suggestion that you should not use one culture's aesthetic values to evaluate another culture, nor can all aesthetic criteria be applied to every art form or ethnic group. This is the dilemma posed in discussions of Black aesthetics or African-American aesthetics. Criteria should be established by those people who create the art.

For Merriam, "The western concept of the aesthetic is the manipulation of form for its own sake. . . . music is treated as an abstract thing in itself."[5] The idea that music sound can evoke an emotional response is culture specific. One can assign the idea of beauty to the art product or the process.[6] Not that beauty is art or art must be beautiful, or that they are the same thing, but there is always a connection. In many instances, "The Western artist sets out with the deliberate intention of creating an object or sound which will be aesthetically admired by those who view or hear it . . ."[7]

People of African descent living in other cultural environments have additional possibilities to express or verbalize a Black aesthetic. Literature is one means for this expression. Augustine N. Mensah said, "The refusal of a black writer to avail himself of the resources of that language (English), that tradition which is not his own, means a failure to utilize a very significant part of the means available, indeed a failure to express an important part of his experience."[?] When available, technological developments can become a significant contributor to aesthetic thought and process, just as a foreign language can be a resource. Innovations, new materials, or the depletion of older resources have given rise to new developments. Cultural aesthetics are developed through personal experience, communication (verbal or otherwise), and community consensus.

In 1973, when speaking of earlier Black writers, African writer Pio Zirimu said, ". . . black people have been and continue to be a nation within a nation—at least culturally, (and) artistically—but without the rights of a nation. They have been a distinct society especially in their authentic creative work." A plurality in artistic evaluation came about as black writers concerned themselves with evaluating their work as African-Americans with a western standard. The 1930s saw the rise of an attitude among a few social academic circles labeled Negritude.[8] Molefi Kete Asante and other similar thinkers have in the 1980s expanded the positive implications of self-determination and use the phrase "Afrocentricity." In Afrocentric thought, it matters not whether the criteria for self-definition are derived from any one African culture. What can be identified among all of the peoples of Africa and their descendants is a common way of thinking. As Asante explains:

> African culture is therefore determined by unity of origin as well as
> a common struggle. All of the African people who participated
> in the mechanized interaction with Europe, and who colored the
> character of Europe while being changed themselves, share
> a commonality.[9]

While this book does not attempt to explain an aesthetic that is all inclusive, we will investigate the aesthetic viewpoints held by African-Americans in the United States who have chosen to drum and dance Mandiani and other Mande music and dance as their personal means of aesthetic expression.

African Music and Dance in the United States: A Brief History

African or Afrocentric music and dance has existed in the United States in the creative processes and approaches to movement exhibited among African-Americans since their arrival more than three hundred years ago. It is suggested by Ivan Van Sertima, author of *They Came Before Columbus*(1970), that Africans were in the Americas even before the early European explorers. Unfortunately there is no continuous record of these early African travelers. One possible source for documented information about Africans brought to the Americas is *The Atlantic Slave Trade, A Census* written in 1969 by Philip Curtin, but music and dance are not specifically considered. Early shipping records were used to determine ports of departure, but identifying cultural background or ethnicity is problematic because many of those ports were staging points where many ethnic groups were held.

The written history of the Americas gives various descriptions and examples of an emerging African-American society, one that exists in conjunction with and that has absorbed a great deal from European-American society. There is documented material that suggests the presentation of African music and dance in the late nineteenth century. Marshall Stearns comments in *The Story of Jazz*(1956) that the minstrel shows of the 1800s featured, among other things, the "African Village." These are entertainment forms which demonstrated the American and European "curiosity for the exotic," as it was often called. However, these presentations were no more than parodies of African village life. Eileen Southern's description of Pinkster Celebrations and John Conny Festivals in *The Music of Black Americans*(1983) suggests these events were mounted in very informal settings. Certainly, many of these "performances" retained traces of African music and dance. But through the early years of African-American existence, the social and political environment in the United States held to the opinion that "African" style performances and activities were not to be sanctioned. Colonialism in Africa from the late nineteenth century also promoted an awareness of African culture in Europe and North America but often did not view the artistic output of these cultures with respect.

Staged performances suggesting African culture were seen on a limited basis from the late 1800s. Photographer Carl Van Vechten, in relating to the work of Nigerian performer Asadata Dafora Horton in 1934, makes reference to writers and journalists who drew parallels between Horton's performance of Kykunkor, a Black ballet opera, and the earlier appearance of the "Dahomey Dancers" at the Chicago World's Fair of 1893. There are no descriptive narratives written by African-Americans on either of these events. Photographs of Horton are possibly the clearest indication of what African-Americans might have seen or participated in as part of the Dance-Opera Kykunkor.

During the "Back to Africa" movement in the early twentieth century led by Marcus Garvey, there were missionaries from the United States moving to Africa. There were also Africans brought to the United States for missionary training. It is quite plausible that these students also had occasion to display their abilities in music and dance. During the 1920s and 30s, a center for creativity within the African-American community existed in Harlem, New York. This location attracted world attention to African-American art and artists. By the time Katherine Dunham's 1940 dance company was established in New York, and Pearl Primus arrived in 1943, both women were accepted by the western arts community. Both of these women were responsible for forming dance companies that, along with western oriented dance programs, presented concert versions of African styled dance. With the arrival of Babatunde Olatunji in 1950, African drumming and dancing with an African director had begun in the United States. With later appearances of national companies from Mali, Ghana, Guinea, and Sénégal the presence of traditional and "neo-traditional" African performance practices were well established.

In a popular sense, African-American involvement in African music and dance is relatively new. As American performers or performing groups made visits to Africa in the 1950s and 60s, and as Africans traveled to the United States in ever increasing numbers, new insights on African performance practices were revealed, and the general interest in African cultures increased. The general approach to African Music and dance was summarized by Melvin Deal as he commented on the dance of Dunham and Primus by saying, "Of course when they did the dances here, they Eurocised them."[10] With Babatunde Olatunji and the formation of his Institute for the Study of African Culture, there was a center created in the United States for the study of African music and dance. Olatunji enlisted the services of djimbe (also spelled djembe[11]) drummer Ladji Camara from Guinea, who came to the United States to perform with the Bambos African Dance Company in Hollywood, California, and other performers from North America and the Caribbean. Many other organizations sprang from Olatunji's institute, such as those created by his early students Arthur Hall and Melvin Deal, for the purpose of training individuals in the art of African drum and dance in the United States. African music and dance styles and similar music and dance forms from the African diaspora are now well represented in the United States. Prominent African music and dance cultures represent countries such as Ghana, Nigeria, Congo, Zaire, Sénégal, Gambia, Mali, and Guinea to name a few. From the Americas, cultures of Cuba, Puerto Rico, Trinidad, Jamaica, Brazil, and others have influenced Africans and African-Americans as well.

The African styled music and dance heard and practiced in the United States until the 1950s was basically from the Yoruba culture via Cuba and Haiti. In the mid-1950s a dance company from Guinea directed by Fodeba Keita performed in New York City and brought dances of the Mande to North America. The number of Africans living in the United States has grown steadily, particularly in New York City. Harlem, New York is frequently referred to as Little Africa. It was Ladji Camara who reportedly brought the first djimbe drum to performers in the United States while he lived and performed in New York City. He is regarded as the first teacher of the djimbe, Mande culture, their dances and songs in the United States. Mandiani has become one of the most recognizable African dances performed by African-Americans.

✳   ✳   ✳

The material in this book has been prepared and organized to give the reader a sense of the music and dance called Mandiani in traditional and contemporary Mande culture. Chapter Two, *Mandiani in West Africa*, provides an overview of Mandiani, djimbe drumming and dancing, and other characteristics of Mandiani such as singing style, dance movements and clothing. Chapter Three, *Mandiani in the United States*, presents Mandiani as it is realized by African-Americans. Chapter Four, *The Psychological Aesthetic*, is a discourse on issues of aesthetic thought surrounding the African-American interpretation of Mandiani. The implications found here extend beyond music and dance and apply to the broader topic of Black aesthetics. It is my sincere wish that this information will make a significant contribution to the study of cultural aesthetics, and most especially to aesthetic understanding throughout the African diaspora.

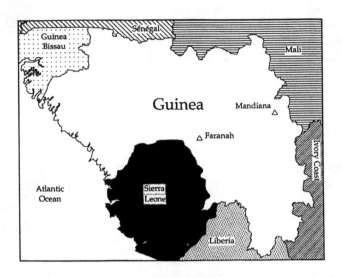

Figure 2.1
Regional Map of Guinea.

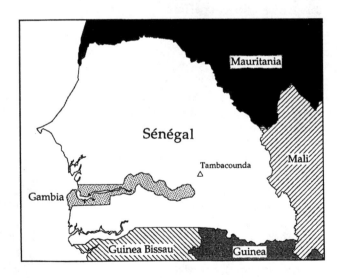

Figure 2.2
Regional Map of Sénégal.

Chapter Two

Mandiani
in West Africa

Mandiani is believed to have originated in the northeast corner of the country now known as Guinea. This community is known as Mandiana. Basory Ibrahima Bangoura, formerly of the national ballet companies of Guinea and Sénégal, as well as many other drummers and dancers from or associated with performers from Guinea, suggest Guinea as Mandiani's place of origin.

The djimbe,[1] a goblet shaped hand drum, is also said to have originated in Guinea among the Malinke in the north. This drum is celebrated for its high, crisp sound by many ethnic groups in this section of West Africa. The Malinke migrated to an area within the Mali Empire around the ninth century A.D. The Diulas of Mali, a branch of the Bambara (Bamana),[2] are known primarily as tradesman and are probably responsible for the spread of this instrument beyond that first migration. According to M'Bemba Bangoura, the djimbe ensemble originated in the Faranah region of Guinea, along what is now the Sierra Leone border. Faranah and Mandiana are shown in *Figure 2.1* as part of the contemporary administrative regions of Guinea. The region known for djimbe drumming in Sénégal, formely called Sénégal Oriental, is now called Tambacounda after its capital and is shown in *Figure 2.2*. According to Pape Moussa Diop, one of the senior historians of Tambacounda, the djimbe is a Bambara instrument originating in Wosolo. This opinion is shared by others from Mali as well. These discrepencies in the point of origin for this drum can be rationalized as the product of regional prejudices and local history. According to Pape Diop, the only drum

19

Figure 2.3
Mandiani Song.

used in the original ensemble was the djimbe and featured four drums only. He believes djimbe in its present shape was brought to these people by a hunter who came upon a spirit playing this drum in the woods.

The double headed cylindrical drums found in the contemporary ensembles of Guinea are known by three names, doun doun or doun-doumba, sangbé, and kenkeni depending on the size and musical role of the individual instrument. The origins of this drum are difficult to trace because it arrived in different regions at different times. According to Omar Thiam, the predecessor of the diun diun in Sénégal may be a drum known as the Xine. This is a small cylindrical drum with one head. Two headed cylindrical drums are found all over West Africa. Cheikh Anta Diop referred to a band of musicians who were part of the army during the Songhai Empire. " They used a war drum . . . called the Djung-Djung."[3]

Song and Singing

Songs are an integral component of the music in most African cultures, and they are a part of Mandiani performances in their social context. In the liner notes for *Rhythms of the Manding* Mondet and Drame mentioned a song being sung in the version of Mandiani which they viewed in a Sénégalese village but did not discuss song text. "The songs (used for Mandiani) are ancient in origin and rarely retain the original text. The art of text improvisation is important and text can be changed to fit the occasion."[4] In staged performances of Mandiani by Africans observed in Africa and the United States, songs are rarely used. However, in a performing group observed in Tambacounda, Mandiani was part of a suite of dances which was prefaced by singing. It was not likely that any of the songs could be assigned to Mandiani alone. The previous song was suggested by two Sénégalese performers. *Figure 2.3* is in the Bambara (Bamana) language spoken in Mali. Assane Konte, born in the Cassamance Region of Sénégal, offered this version. This is an agricultural song used after a day's work in the fields or following the harvest. The song is sung in the call and response mode.

Although text and melody vary from song to song, there are characteristics which are common among the songs suggested for Mandiani. The melodic characteristics associated with these songs and the singing style include: 1) one or more intervals of a perfect fourth or fifth when the melody moves upward. Descending melody lines usually move in a scale-like manner; 2) these melodies are rarely "harmonized" in the western sense. Occasionally, one chorus singer might vary from the established response pattern creating incidental harmony for a brief moment; 3) the melodic line or vocal phrase is rarely very long; 4) the song is sung at a pitch level comfortable enough for most of the participants to sing in the upper end of their vocal range allowing for a very forceful sound; 5) songs sung in call and response fashion have one song leader with the remaining participants responding; and 6) any vocal improvisations are performed by the soloist/song leader. Although examples of songs that alternate according to gender were heard in many instances, the Mandiani songs which I heard did not fall into this category.

Age, Gender, and Occasion for Mandiani in Africa

During community and social events I observed in Sénégal near Dakar, all ages participated in the dancing. Differences did not occur in the basic movement performed in Mandiani. Young people's dance was differentiated in that it had a greater variety and a more vigorous manner of presentation. For example, the tempo might accelerate for a younger dancer. Nonetheless, the basic movements remained the same for all ages. For the older age groups, the movements were simply executed in a more conservative manner and at a comfortable tempo for the dancer. Demonstrations were offered and observed to show how an elder might perform the dance. It was also pointed out that an elder drummer might use a smaller or lighter instrument, or play the drum from a seated position. When playing, the elder musician might also choose a time-keeping rhythm rather than the lead role. If he believed the younger player would benefit from clarification in a particular aspect of the music, this would take place outside of and away from the performance arena.

Among the drummers and dancers from Guinea, Tambacounda, and Dakar, Sénégal, there was a gender reference for the dance Mandiani when we discussed dances apart from the event. M'Bemba Bangoura stated that for his generation Mandiani is a dance performed by young girls. One occasion is after completing their initiation into the adult world. There are at least two written references to Mandiani as a dance for women only: 1) the explanation provided by the Guinea Ballet during their 1991 United States tour. Mandiani was described as a puberty dance performed by young maidens who were trained to perform this dance for special ceremonial occasions only; and 2) music researcher Bernard Mondet, and djimbe drummer Adama Drame, described occasions where Mandiani is danced this way:

> Dances start with a song chanted by a woman, which is then taken up by the spectators in chorus.

> For a wedding, the jembe is played each day for seven to ten days, for several hours at a time, either during the day or in the evening. On these occasions only women or young girls dance. The bridal couple is never present, nor are the respective mothers, who are represented by women chosen from among the friends of the family.[5]

In the folkloric companies touring the United States from the Mande regions, there are close to an equal number of male and female dancers. The drummers, kora, balafon, and flute players are generally males. There is also a featured singer, often female. The repertoire generally depicts social dances and occasionally dances assembled to suggest legend and/or ritual. The social dancing of men represented in these performances is usually acrobatic in nature, displaying feats of strength or agility. Female movements can be slow, graceful and flowing, or quick and athletic requiring great agility. Assane Konte called Mandiani "a happiness dance." Malang Bayo, formerly of the National Ballet of Sénégal, used the same words in relating the spirit in which the dance is performed. He offered an example of how the dance might commence in the village:

There may have been a time historically when there was no rain and then there was rain and the people danced Mandiani. In the village, one person will start the dance. As the dance leader forms a circle, it is up to those who join in to follow the dance leader in each basic dance step or movement.

M'Bemba Bangoura, Basory Bangoura, and Mor Thiam only alluded to the use of Mandiani as a spiritual dance. M'Bemba comments, "Maybe the old people know about such a thing but it is not that way now." Mor Thiam suggested that long ago Mandiani was danced during the second of three stages leading to spirit possession but that practice no longer exists. In contemporary society, Mandiani is considered a social dance. I asked Pape Diop about the meaning of Mandiani long ago and what was thought when Mandiani was danced in the bush. He said that in the bush, Mandiani was the dance of the panther and mimicked its movements. When danced, it was a dance for celebrating.

The Dance

Dance in most African societies has basic movement characteristics and recognizable gestures which can be used to identify a culture. Communities throughout the continent will display their distinct cultural signature through movement styles or specific features, for example, the arm motions of the Ewe people of Ghana and Togo resemble the movements of a folded bird's wing, or the erect and otherwise motionless leaps of the Masai from Kenya are easily recognized as unique to their ethnic group. Careful observers might also recognize each dancer's personal touch or style even when there are many dancers performing the same movement. By looking at a variety of dances, one might eventually recognize which movements are clearly part of the culture or ethnic group and also which movements might be unique to one dance. The following are my observations of Mande dance and more specifically, Mandiani.

Posture

At the root of all dance movement is posture. The basic posture for the dance Mandiani is knees bent with the upper body inclined forward at the waist. Dancers with formal western training would refer to this position as a forward pelvic tilt. This posture is not unique to the Mande. It can be found in many cultures and is often the result of common approaches to similar activities such as those found in farming or the way many women stand while cooking in rural communities. Since a basic posture for dance is developed over many generations and it is perpetuated through simple observation and imitation, it tends to become fixed in a community. In creating new movements or new dances, a basic vocabulary of gestures is used. These signature movements may be repeated, augmented, abbreviated, or compressed, but they will remain recognizable. The catalog of completely different gestures, or movements recognized as belonging to distinctly different dances may be limited. Dances performed by people living by the sea might have gestures resembling the act of fishing or casting nets, and those who sustain themselves by farming may use movements depicting an agrarian existence. Hunters and herders often limit their movement styles to occupational movements.

Rhythm in Movement

The "triplet" is a rapid three step sequence seen in the dance Mandiani. When used by dancer and dance ethnographer Kariamu Welsh Asante, the word triplet simply refers to three quick foot steps. These steps do not necessarily conform to the strict musical definition of a triplet. *Figure 2.4* (Examples A and B) illustrates the resultant rhythms in this foot pattern. Example A represents the triplet over the first half of the bar (the first two dotted quarter notes) when danced in 12/8 meter.

Because of the speed and control required to execute this movement in Mandiani, the rhythmic subdivision can change based on the tempo. *Figure 2.4* represents three rhythmic articulations that are used in the variety of tempos used for Mandiani. Example A represents the rhythmic articulation created by the foot movements of Mandiani at a moderate tempo (dotted quarter note = 150). Example B represents the rhythmic articulation of the feet as Mandiani is taught in the United States. The movement is also articulated this way at a faster performance tempo (dotted quarter note = 180). Example C represents the rhythm articulated by many African-Americans as they execute the movement through a range of tempos (dotted quarter note = 150-190). Note that the dotted line between counts one and two is used to illustrate a rhythmic pulse that is often counted but not articulated be-

Ex. A Fast foot rhythm as the dance is executed in Africa.

Ex. B Foot rhythm as the dance is taught in the United States.

Ex. C The rhythm as articulated by many African-Americans.

Figure 2.4
Resultant Rhythm in the Mandiani Foot Pattern.

cause the foot does not leave the ground. Also, the rhythmic interpretations of B and C are based in duple rather than triple meter.

A collection of movements which are regularly associated with each other will ultimately be identified as a dance. A perennial question asked about African music and dance is, "what comes first, the music or the dance movement?" This depends on the culture and the dance. One aspect can easily affect the other and does so at various times in many cultures. This question may never be answered for ancient dances such as Mandiani. The name given to a dance can be taken from an event, a place, a drum, or in some instances, a food. The movements are generally connected to that entity, occasion or event. A wide range of variations or departures from established rhythms or movement norms within a dance are easily recognized and generally accepted within the culture. There were a variety of arm and leg movements with variations observed during the dancing of Mandiani, but none of them were referred to consistently as Mandiani movements. The movements discussed in the following section were consistently referred to by informants as basic movements for the dance Mandiani. *Figure 2.5* illustrates the basic step pattern.

Preparatory position beginning with the right foot;

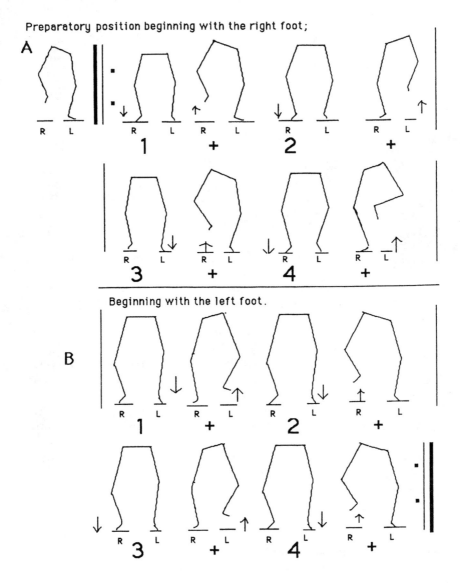

Figure 2.5
The Basic Step Pattern for Mandiani.

Characteristic Mande movement styles may include the following: 1) a sequence of steps which requires the dancer to raise one foot at a time and lower it again. The pattern may occur while standing in one place or while moving from side to side. If the pattern is used for moving from one position in the dance arena to another, the steps occurring on counts 2, 3, and 4 of this illustration allow the dancer to travel with the movement. In *Figure 2.5*, section "A," the step moves the dancer to the right. In section "B," the movement will travel to the left. Moving the dancer forward or backward can also be accomplished at these points in the pattern. The movement cycle is usually performed in even numbered repetitions; 2) the dancer carries his or her weight on the balls of the feet with the heel barely off the ground. *Figure 2.5* also suggests this basic stance; 3) this movement may be executed with such intensity that the dancer is propelled completely off the ground. The lift normally occurs between counts one and two of this illustration. The body is usually in a contracted position when the lift occurs; 4) in this illustration the triplet begins on count one and ends on count two. The rhythm created in this part of the step may vary depending on the dance tempo (*see Figure 2.4*).

There are several variations of this movement which also illustrate arm extension.[6] *Figure 2.6* combines the basic foot pattern and one suggested arm movement identified as a Mandiani gesture. The basic version illustrated here was presented by Bayo. When this movement starts with count one on the right foot, the arms circle in front of the body in a clockwise direction. When count one begins with the left foot the arms circle counter clockwise. The hands actually pass each other in front of the chest at count three. *Figures 2.7* and *2.8* illustrate two additional arm variations which have also been recognized as belonging to Mandiani. *Figure 2.7* places the circular motion at the side of the body so that as one views the dancer's profile, the arms resemble two propellers whirling in opposing directions. The hands and arms meet above the dancer's head and reverse direction on count one. The arms make two complete revolutions during the four counts of the movement. *Figure 2.8* suggests another variation which causes the arms to circle in front of the body, however, they move in parallel motion. M'Bembe Bangoura suggests that in Guinea, as each group of young women returns from their initiation, they probably develop a variation of this basic movement to preserve their group identity. Incorporating movements from other dances is an acceptable realization of one's creativity. These or similar

Figure 2.6
Mandiani as Illustrated by Malang Bayo.

Figure 2.7
Arm Variation, Propeller Motion.

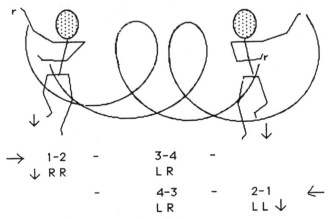

Figure 2.8
Arm Variation, Parallel Motion.

movements may appear in other dances of the Mande culture. They are familiar enough to be considered part of a basic movement vocabulary.

Two additional dances, Domba and Doundoumba, often share this general movement and a variety of musical elements with Mandiani. Doundoumba, however, also has a wide variety of distinctly different movements. The musical elements shared in these three dances will be discussed under the heading *The Music*.

Tempo is the primary factor in determining which dance is being performed and how the Mandiani movement might be executed. The slowest tempo is used for Doundoumba, approximately two pulses per second.[7] This dance is described as a dance of the strong men. Women do not perform dance movements belonging to Doundoumba, according to most Mande informants. In the village this dance is gender specific. For theatrical reasons, it is common to have large numbers of dancers on stage while Doundoumba, Mandiani, and Domba are being performed. In staged productions, when women dance to the music of Doundoumba, they are dancing movements from Mandiani. If men dance to the music of Mandiani, they are probably using Doundoumba movements. Mandiani has a tempo slightly faster than Doundoumba.[8] Domba is the third dance which may share this movement. It is danced at a very fast tempo and is often performed on stage by men and women. Mori Diane, who was working as an artist representative in Tambacounda, said Domba is a Malinke word which was shortened from "dembadon." It is translated to mean "happy mother." This dance was performed by a mother after the first night her daughter spent with her new husband. The mother of the bride would dance this dance when she had verification that her daughter was a virgin.

Since the selected movements can be shared by all three dances yet were identified as belonging to Mandiani, I asked my informants how others can distinguish one dance from another. Malang Bayo used the position of the arms to distinguish the difference between Domba and Mandiani. According to Bayo, the arms for Domba are held chest high (or slightly lower) and extend to the sides without moving in a circle. He continued to described the differences between Domba and Mandiani by saying,

> One difference is in the position of the hands for Domba. The arms are low, held close to the body with the palms facing downward and a twist in the lower torso. Mandiani has the hands open and facing outward (with no twist in the torso) and the steps can move from side to side.

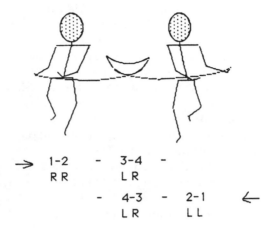

$$\rightarrow \quad \begin{array}{ccc} 1\text{-}2 & - & 3\text{-}4 \\ R\,R & & L\,R \end{array} \quad -$$

$$- \quad \begin{array}{ccc} 4\text{-}3 & - & 2\text{-}1 \\ L\,R & & L\,L \end{array} \quad \leftarrow$$

Figure 2.9
Arm Motion for Domba.

When observing Bayo execute the movement the Domba tempo was so fast it seemed to have a limiting effect on the range of arm motion. *Figure 2.9* shows the arm movement used by Bayo to identify Domba. Bayo also corroborated the statement that men do not dance Mandiani as illustrated in *Figures 2.6, 2.7,* and *2.8.* This understood, he continued by saying if he did dance Mandiani he would execute the movements as illustrated. The primary difference between Bayo's examples of Mandiani and the same movements danced to the Doundoumba rhythm was that while dancing Doundoumba at the slower tempo, he appeared to spend much more time suspended in midair. When Mandiani movements are performed at the slower tempo for Doundoumba, many individual interpretations may result. When men perform Doundoumba at the faster tempo for Mandiani, their movements may lose definition and impact.

A significant difference in the way men and women perform these dances shows in the way the hands are held during the dance. Men usually dance Doundoumba with their hands clenched in a fist; women generally dance Mandiani with their hands open. Exceptions to this rule have been noted in Doundoumba but not in Mandiani. Within the character of the dance Doundoumba, male dancers often show their strength by using very quick and percussive movements. Because male dancers typically do not appear soft or sinuous while dancing, the movements generally used by males appear quite angular. When Domba is performed at its normal speed, it is difficult to fully extend or rotate the limbs as when Domba is danced to the Mandiani rhythm. Consequently, Domba movements are neither fully contracted nor fully extended when danced at normal speed.

Variation and improvisation take place among dancers when they step into the center of the dance arena. The circle is a primary configuration for social dances and individuals will step into the center of the circle to execute a variation of the dance movement being performed or a separate movement unlike the rest of the dancing group. At that time, the principal drummer will bring the music to a higher level of intensity to encourage the solo dancer or group of soloists. The movements performed during the "solo" are developed by each dancer individually, but these movements are generally a version of the basic dance movement being executed by the collective group dancing. Soloists gain distinction for their interpretations of movement.

The Instruments

The djimbe can be found throughout the Mande populations of West Africa. Its presence in Guinea and Mali has already been discussed. Although the Sénégalese were aware of the djimbe in regions beyond Tambacounda, it was not given serious attention throughout the country until Fodeba Keita and the formation of the Sénégalese National Ballet Company in the mid-1950s following Sénégal's independence. Within the many ethnic groups of Sénégal, the djimbe is now unquestionably an integral part of contemporary society. This drum can also be found in Côte D'Ivoire, Burkina Faso, Sierra Leone, Liberia, and The Gambia.

The instrument used to complement the djimbe in Guinea is called the doundoun, and in Sénégal it is called the diun diun. This drum provides the prominent bass frequencies and rhythms in the drum ensemble. The names are derived from the sound which emanates from the drum as it is played. In contemporary culture, the doundoun and diun diun are fashioned from steel drums, some as large as 55 gallons. Historically, all of the drums, the djimbe, doundoun, and diun diun were carved from a solid piece of wood. When constructing a contemporary three drum set, the sangbé is made from a metal drum which is slightly smaller than the doundoun and usually produces a second bass or counter bass drum rhythm. In some instances, it functions in the same role as the doundoun with a slightly higher pitch. The kenkeni is the smallest of the three drums and provides another intermediate rhythm. It has a sound pitched between the djimbe and the sangbé. Attached to the sangbé is a metal bell similar in sound to the Latin cowbell. The bell is played with a metal rod, or, it is hand held and played with a metal ring around one finger or a short metal rod. This bell is always played by the drummers of Guinea, but is not regularly used by drummers in Sénégal and Mali. I have never seen the bell played as a single instrument but it does not seen unlikely for it to be played as such.

There are several small hand held rattles which are sometimes used to accompany the djimbe ensemble. Basket rattles were seen in use during presentations by the Guinea Ballet during their United States tour of 1990. These instruments were played in sets of two, usually by female dancers, or on occasion by men when there were only male musicians on stage. The Guinea Ballet describes this instrument as a "Small gourd containing pebbles, which is attached to the end of a stick and when shaken produces a sharp clicking sound, rather like maracas, although popularly referred to in Guinea as 'castanets.' The small gourd is normally decorated with beads and raffia." *Figure 2.10* shows a representation of these small rattles called "castanets." Another instrument used in Guinea to produce a similar high crisp sound is called the "wasa wombe" by Basory Bangoura. The wasa wombe is made with a series of seven to nine small calabash disks graduated from approximately two to four inches in diameter. A hole is drilled in the center of each disk, and they are arranged on a hand held "L" shaped stick.[9] *Figure 2.11* shows the wasa wombe which is normally played in pairs. A third instrument in Guinea and in Sénégal is the calabash itself. It may range in size from one foot to three feet in diameter and is played with the hands. Metal rings are placed on the fingers to create a crackling sound. The gourd can be cut into two halves or played whole.

The djimbe can also wear sound enhancing devices called kesingkesings in the Wolof language. This term mimics the sound made when the drum is struck. In Bambara, the term used is gnagnama, pronounced "nyanyama." The word means "ear" and relates to the possible appearance of these fan or triangular shaped metal sheets which are usually affixed to the top edge of the djimbe with rope or cord in sets of two or three. Each sheet has a series of holes around the outer edge with metal rings inserted. Bambara women are known to pierce the ear many times around the outer edge. The metal sheets vibrate when the drum is struck according to the force and type of stroke delivered by the player. One diun diun player in Sénégal used a kesingkesing attached to his drum and played it instead of a bell. *Figure 2.12* shows a djimbe with gnagnama attached.

This sound enhancement is consistent with the concept of African sound aesthetics presented by other authors (Nketia 1974, and Bebey 1984) who state that in the African aesthetic, a pure tone or one dimensional sound is not always a beautiful sound, or, it may not be the preferred sound at that instant. Mor Thiam suggests that the sound created by the devices also serves to stabilize the musical time. This additional sound only sustains for a split second and provides a high distinguishable buzz. The musicians and dancers can use this sound to synchronize their playing. I have seen many instruments in the Mande cultures with added materials that buzzed, jingled, or rattled as the instrument is played. They also effectively mark the strong pulses in the music as the instrument is played.

Shape, Size and Sound of the Drums

The primary structural components of the djimbe are the "bowl" and the "stem" or "pipe." The interior shape of the bowl, both in depth and width, will determine the pitch of the primary open tone. The depth and curve at the base of the bowl will determine the reflected high pitch of the "slap." The width of the hole at the base of the bowl and the length and slope of the interior pipe walls will determine the resonance of the "bass" tone. The length of the stem or pipe and bowl combined will determine bass frequency. With the drum in its normal playing range, head tension is a minor variable. Tone production and technique will be discussed later in this chapter. An average drum from Guinea is approximately 15 to 18 inches tall. With a straight pipe, the bass tone of a drum that size vibrates between 69.2956 and 73.4161 Hz when tuned appropriately for the music sound of Guinea. If the pipe of the drum has a conical interior wall varying from 7 inches at the bottom to 5 inches at the base of the bowl, the bass resonance will be slightly higher. The bowl diameter and head tension will determine the open tone of the drum. The average Guinea drum's bowl diameter is 12 inches or less. With the typical high tensioning used, the tone is also higher.

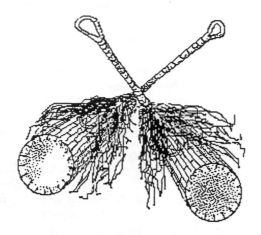

Figure 2.10
Basket Rattles called Castanets.

Figure 2.11
The Wasa Wombe.

Figure 2.12 *Djimbe with
Kesingkesings Attached.*

From observations over several years, a basic hypothesis to explain a culture-based preference in drum size was verified by drummers from Guinea. The head diameters of Guinean drums are typically the smallest of the djimbe playing communities. The pipes tend to be cylindrical and the bowls shorter than drums from other countries. The drummers of Mali have the instruments with the largest drumhead diameter, bowl depth, and pipe length. Sénégalese drums fall somewhere between the two, although there are some rare exceptions to the standard instuments. These structural factors become apparent in the sound of drum ensembles from various regions.

To produce the three prominent sounds noted earlier, hand technique is critical. The highest sound, or slap, associated with the instrument is achieved by striking the drumhead with the fingers slightly separated. The full length of the fingers contacts the top edge of the drum. The palm should not. The focus of the blow is directed to the ends of the fingers in order to isolate the highest harmonics in the vibrating pattern of the drumhead.[10] One possible alternative for an occasional solo sound resembles a technique used on the conga drum. This requires one hand to mute the drumhead, while the other strikes the head, producing the slap. This sound is considerably less resonant but sounds like a gun shot. The second sound is commonly called the "tone." This sound is achieved when all four fingers strike the drumhead flatly at the rim and extend to their full-length in contact with the drumhead. The tone produced equates to the mid-range of the drum's sound spectrum. A variation of this sound is achieved when the player leaves the fingers in contact with the drumhead to produce a very "dry" or muted tone. The third sound is the bass or lowest frequency of the drum. This sound is achieved by striking the drumhead at or near the center with the entire hand. Several of the African players I observed preferred to strike the drum near the edge using the base of the fingers held flat and together. This technique reduces the movement required to place the palm in the center of the drum. It also diminishes the probability of pushing the drum "out of tune." *Figure 2.13* shows the basic hand position for each of the three prominent sounds produced on the djimbe.[11]

Recorded and live performances of Mande musicians provide the basis for the following evaluations. The bass sound is not heard prominently in many recorded examples or live performances of Guinean djimbe playing. However, the recordings of djimbe playing from Mali suggest the use of the bass tone is quite prominent in their music. In

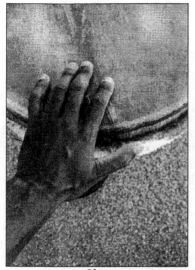

Slap

Tone

Bass

Figure 2.13
The Basic Hand Positions for Three Prominent Djimbe Sounds.

recorded and live examples of Guinean drummers, the slap is the dominant sound for solo playing and the open tone along with the slap are dominant in accompaniment parts. The Sénégalese drummers use a variety of sounds suggesting less emphasis on the slap sound. The perceived sound spectrum of the Guinea drummers is the highest in registration, and the sound of Mali drummers is the lowest. It is difficult to quantify these observations because it would require larger samples than are available. However, these same observations have been made by many of the drummers involved in this study.

The Guinea drum ensembles exploit the lower frequency range by using three different sizes of the two-headed drum (doundoun) in interlocking rhythm combinations. In the music heard from Mali and Sénégal, there was usually only one two headed drum. One ensemble in Sénégal used a diun diun and a steel drum with one head which was played by hand. Perhaps sufficient variety is achieved in the djimbe "part playing" from these two regions. Instead of having three double-headed drums creating varied melodic parts below the soloist, similar results are achieved in the bass tones played by the accompanying djimbe drums.

Materials and Construction

In Guinea the djimbe is carved from trees in the redwood family. After a performance in Scottsdale, Arizona, Guinean drummers performing with the touring company Africa Oye identified Disolo as the wood preferred by their contemporary master drummers. Traditional woods used in Mali are Tali and Coba. Kekho, Lingo, and Bimbekahagna are preferred now because the wood is not as heavy. The traditional wood used in Sénégal is Dimba. Because of its dense nature, drums made from Dimba can be rather heavy. Among contemporary djimbe drummers in West Africa and the United States, alternative woods are sought. Mango, Nime, Gertetoubape, and Kélé are now being used in Sénégal as alternatives. These lighter woods lessen the weight of the djimbe.

The playing surfaces of the djimbe and diun diun require separate considerations. For the djimbe, goat skin is the most commonly used material. According to Pape Diop, the hide of a female goat is best. Before goat, antelope skins were the norm. Current trends seem to suggest thin calf skin as a durable alternative to goat skin for the djimbe. These animal hides are left raw and unprocessed. The fat must be carefully removed from the underside of the hide. The use of salt as a curing agent is sometimes necessary, but most drummers prefer to have the skins mounted on the drums immediately after removing it from the animal. At that time the skin is very pliable and easily manipulated during the mounting process. If it is necessary to store a skin before using it, the skin should be dried in as natural a state as possible.

The thickness and density of the skin is important. The thinner the skin, the more resonant it will be. Therefore, thin skins are better suited for the djimbe. The diun diun can accept a thicker hide. The hair on the playing surface must be removed from those skins to be used on the djimbe. This is normally done with a razor blade or very sharp knife. Care must be taken to avoid nicking or puncturing the animal skin. On the other hand, the diun diun, or doundoun, sangbé, and kenkeni require a less resonant drumhead. Many contemporary drummers use cowhide because it is usually thicker and less resonant. An alternative solution first observed in Dakar, Sénégal, was to leave a quantity of hair on the playing surface of the goat skin when used for the diun diun. By doing so, the desired minimum resonance was achieved.

All of these drums were originally assembled with a minimum of hardware and tools. The lacing material was regularly made from hide. Various vines or similar materials were used for mounting rings. It was expected that a drum could be assembled with available raw materials. One of the early modifications to this process was the use of a double ring system which eliminated the need to insert lacing holes in the animal skin. A ring placed over the animal skin was laced to a second ring at the base of the drum bowl. Synthetic cord has been adopted for the lacing process. This technique creates a nesting ring at the top and bottom of the djimbe bowl and on either side of the diun diun. Low stretch nylon cord is available in a variety of colors and is often used for its decorative potential. Listed below are the procedures followed in preparing and mounting the drumhead on the djimbe or diun diun.

① If the skin has not just been removed from the animal, you must soak the dried skin until it is very pliable, usually four or five hours. At this point the hair may be removed with a sharp blade the same way one might shave with a razor but without using shaving cream or lather. You may also wait until the skin is mounted and dry. By waiting to shave just the playing surface, a decorative collar of hair may be left around the edge of the drum overlapping the top nesting ring.

② Prepare the nesting rings by creating anchoring loops using three or four millimeter cord. One large ring for the top of the drum, and a smaller one that will just slip over the bottom pipe. The knots should be spaced the knots one to three inches apart. Each ring must have the same number of knots. The most common knot used is called the Lark's Head (see *Figure 2.14, A*).

③ Place the animal skin over the drum shell, overlay the first ring (the large one without anchoring loops), and fold the animal skin up and over the top of the drum (see *Figure 2.14, B, C, D*).

④ Install the lower nesting ring by slipping it over the tail of the drum. An alternative is to have this lower ring welded while around the drum at the base of the bowl. In that event, the knots will be tied with the ring in that position. The second nesting ring which secures the drumhead to the drum will be placed over the folded up animal skin (see *Figure 2.14, E 1*).

⑤ While the animal skin is still wet, initiate the vertical lace by securing the end of the cord at one point and continue lacing up and down (top to bottom) until all the loops of the nesting rings have been used (see *Figure 2.14, E 2*).

⑥ Pull each vertical section to apply pressure to the animal skin(s) evenly and tie off the excess cord. Do not attempt to tune the drum to its playing range at this time. You may need to repeat this pulling phase several times after a two day drying period (see *Figure 2.14, F*).

⑦ Horizontal lacing is used for the final tuning. This may require two or more revolutions to provide the proper tension (see *Figure 2.14, G 1, 2, 3*).

Figure 2.14, views "A" through "G," illustrates one standard procedure used for lacing the djimbe. View "A" shows the knots used to prepare the nesting ring. Views "B" through "G," show how to attach the skin to the drum. *Figure 2.15*, views "A" through "G," illustrates the same system used for the diun diun. There are alternative systems used, but this one has been seen in a variety of settings. The drum skins for the diun diun may be goat or cow skin and they are prepared in the same manner as those used on the djimbe. If dried, they must be soaked until pliable. The difference between preparing the diun diun and preparing the djimbe is that four rings must be prepared for the diun diun. Each end of the drum must have knots for lacing the drum. Instead of the lower ring resting against the bowl of the drum as with the djimbe, the second ring is positioned so that when you lace the drum, you are pulling on the opposing nesting ring and drumhead.

Two issues are of great concern to many players after assembling the drum and have some bearing on the way an individual player might approach the assembly process. The first involves the physical appearance of the instrument. Most of the drums seen in Sénégal which were used by Sénégalese musicians did not retain the excess skin folded over the top nesting ring. The skin was positioned so that the top ring was at least one and one half inches below the top of the drum. This may have been done to more easily accommodate the mounting of kesingkesings. Most of these sound enhancers are constructed with a rigid stem attached. This stem is inserted through one of the loops created by the cord on the nesting ring and then wedged between the cord around the drum and the drum shell.

The second possibility is that the final fold of skin is not important to the drummer's aesthetic viewpoint, or, stability after tuning the drum is a concern of higher priority. If the skin is mounted with the hair on, the playing surface is shaved but the hair is untouched on the final fold. This visual concern may subsequently impact the ability of the drum to hold rope tension after tuning. From a purely functional standpoint, if the hair remains on that portion of the skin which weaves through the rings, it may increase the likelihood of the drum head slipping through the rings and thus require the drum to be tuned more frequently. If the hair is removed before mounting, the likelihood of the animal hide slipping may be diminished but not totally eliminated.

A contemporary alternative was first seen used by Gueye in the United States. The first two rings were mounted just as the two rings at the top of the drum in *Figure 2.14*. The third ring was the nesting ring. In this case the skin was folded around ring one, between rings one and two, and then folded over ring two. The final fold covered both rings and was trimmed just below the first. The third ring, or nesting ring, was positioned atop rings one and two. With this "S" shaped fold and final section of skin covering both rings, the skin did not slip and consistent tension was retained for a greater period of time.

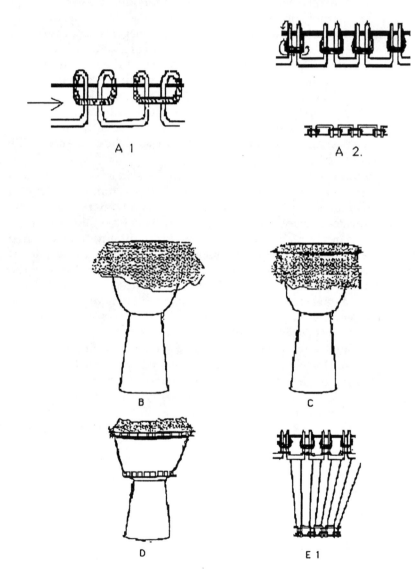

Figure 2.14
The Standard Process for Lacing a Djimbe.

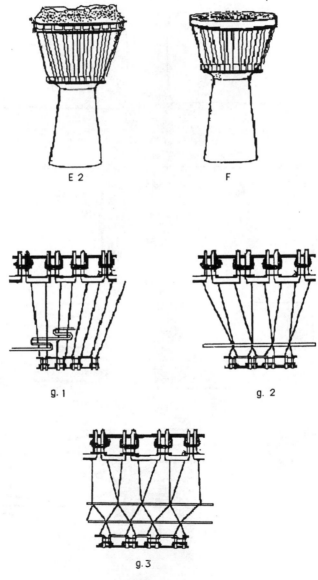

Figure 2.14, continued.

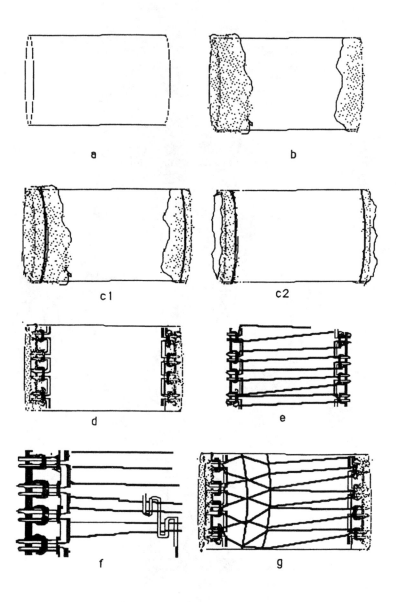

Figure 2.15 *Lacing Process for the Diun Diun.*

Wearing the Drum and Posture

Several factors determine posture for drummers. These are based on the instrument's function, the player's mobility, the desired playing position, body mechanics, and personal comfort. The djimbe is often worn by the player. Historical and contemporary applications often require the drummer to be mobile. Generally the drummer is standing or walking while playing. There are two common systems in use to suspend the drum. With the first approach, a cord or strap is attached near the top edge of the drum and tied around the performer's waist. The strap has a single point of attachment to the drum which allows the stem to fall between the player's legs. According to most drummers, this is the original carrying system. The strap around the waist is the only means of adjusting the playing height of the instrument. The playing surface of the drum will remain fixed where the strap settles. For increased flexibility, the strap can be attached at a lower position on the bowl of the drum or tied loosely so the drumhead rests lower on the player's legs.

The second option is to use a double harness system. The straps are attached near the top of the drum and placed over each shoulder, crossed in back of the musician, brought around the ribs, and connected under the pipe of the djimbe at the base of the bowl. This creates two contact points on the instrument. The position of the drum is then adjustable by lengthening or shortening the strap. While playing, adjustments can be made by varying the tilt of the drum itself since the straps are not tied to the player. Variations have been observed but the basic mechanics remain the same. *Figure 2.16* shows both systems.

The diun diun can be carried with similar systems. The drummer can use a single strap around the waist or over one shoulder with the drum hanging horizontally. This position will allow one hand to play the drumhead and the other to play the bell, should one be attached. The second possibility is to use a double harness approach, much like that used for the djimbe. With this approach, four contact points must be determined. These contact points may be roughly shoulder's width apart. The straps are connected so that the drum is held in a horizontal position in front of the player. The straps are crossed behind the player's back. Height adjustment is regulated by the length of the straps. This method is not very common and is generally reserved for drums that are very heavy. One alternative used by contemporary players is to place the drums on a stand or movable cart. This option is used when the drum is very heavy, or when one player uses multiple drums.

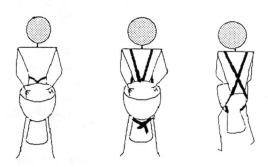

Harness Systems used for Carrying the Djimbe.

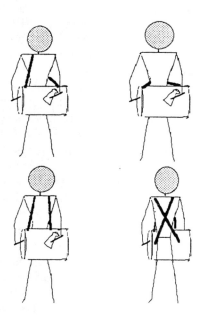

Harness Systems used for Carrying the Diun Diun.

Figure 2.16
Two Harness Systems used for Carrying the Djimbe and Diun Diun.

Figure 2.17
Characteristic Posture for the Djimbe Soloist.

With each method, the drums can be played while standing erect. This is acceptable for accompanying drummers, but is not usual for djimbe soloists. The characteristic posture for the djimbe soloist is shown in *Figure 2.17*, that is, standing with knees bent and feet flat on the ground. The player's weight is supported by the arches and balls of the feet, with the pelvis inclined forward, back arched, the chest pushed forward and open, shoulders back with the head held up. A common variation of this posture is to contract the body to an even greater extent. This squatting position allows the djimbe to rest on the floor or ground, taking the weight of the drum off of the player's shoulders and back.

A variety of playing positions are used by djimbe players to suit their own personalities and talents. Common positions include: a) standing upright; b) standing upright and arching the back slightly while carrying the tail of the drum to either side of the body; c) a kneel-

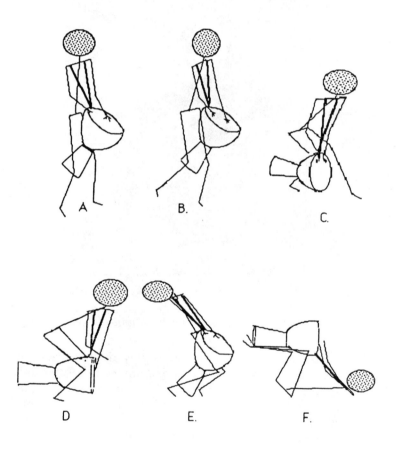

Figure 2.18
Six Possible Djimbe Playing Positions.

ing position which involves bending one's legs so the knee will drop toward the floor while taking a forward step with the other leg. This step ends with the thigh parallel to the floor. The player's torso is either upright or inclined slightly forward. The drum is carried on the same side as the lowered knee; d) in another position the drummer must squat until the drum is resting on the ground. The torso is bent forward with the back arched; e) this view requires a fully arched back and dropping the head backwards as if to rest on the floor; f) this position has the drummer lying on his or her back with knees bent, supporting the drum with the knees and shins. *Figure 2.18*, views "A" through "F," shows each of these possible playing positions.

Rhythms

Signals

Two terms associated with drum based signals in African performance practice are the "call," and the "break." The call has a variety of implications, but it is most certainly associated with direct communication from the lead drummer to the performing group or the community at large. In some instances the call can be a long phrase which begins with the lead drummer. This person is subsequently joined by the remaining drummers in the ensemble to complete the phrase before the dance begins. *Figure 2.19* presents two examples of calls used for Mandiani. Examples A and B are commonly heard in Mande communities. These signals are played to initiate the dance. A signal used as the music progresses is called a "break." When played during the dance it is used as a directive to change the step or movement. Examples A and B can also be used as breaks. The break is played by the lead drummer.

Accompaniment

In today's social setting, Mandiani is usually identified through the music, since music initiates the dance in these settings. As mentioned earlier, Doundounba, Domba and Mandiani are recognized or differentiated through tempo and the rhythms played on the diun diun. The diun diun player is significant because this player is in part responsible for rhythm and tempo accuracy. *Figure 2.20* gives examples of the rhythms used for Doundoumba, Domba, and Mandiani as played by the Mande musicians consulted for this project. In Doundoumba, the doundoun player also fulfills a solo role. This drum is responsible for ar-

Example A

Example B

Figure 2.19
Two Examples of the Call.

ticulating the movements of the dancers. Examples heard performed by
the Guinea ballet in concert featured an ensemble of only the doundoun, sangbé, and kenkeni to accompany this dance.

In any given setting, the parts illustrated are distributed among the
drummers present. One djimbe player must function primarily as
leader. The music played by the lead drummer will vary according to
the dance and/or movements of the dancers. Samples of lead playing
will be given later in this section. Example A.1 is the accompaniment for
Doundoumba as played in Sénégal using three djimbe players. Example
A.2 shows the accompaniment parts for Doundoumba as played by M'-
Bemba Bangoura from Guinea. There are two additional low drum
parts, the sangbé with bell attached, and the kenkeni. This combination
is consistently included in the Guinea drum ensembles when players
are available. Example B is Domba, an example provided by Yacine
Gueye. Mandiani from Guinea (C.2) was demonstrated with eight
djimbe parts, three low drums, and one bell rhythm.

The Sénégalese version of Mandiani shows the common djimbe part
on the first line with its variation shown on line two along with one
other accompanying part. When there were only two djimbe players

Example A.1 Doundoumba–Malang Bayo

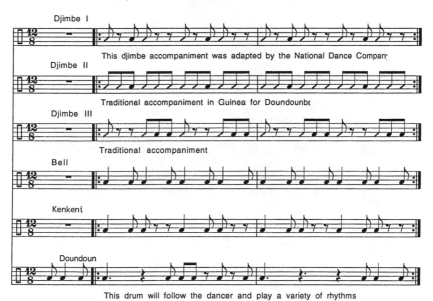

This drum will follow the dancer and play a variety of rhythms

Example A.2 Doundoumba–M'Bemba Bangoura

Figure 2.20
Rhythms used for Doundoumba, Domba and Mandiani.

Example B Domba - Malang Bayo

Example C.1 Mandiani–Malang Bayo

Figure 2.20, *continued.*

Example C.2 Mandiani – M'Bemba Bangoura

Figure 2.20, *continued.*

drumming in Tambacounda, variations which displaced the first articulation by one or two notes were played.[12] The lead drummer or soloist alternated between part playing, solo drumming, or occasionally not playing at all.

The diun diun in Sénégal does not present the wide variety of rhythms normally played for Mandiani, but a few alternatives have been noted. The diun diun part presented in *Example C.1* was offered by Bayo. Konte also offered two variations for the diun diun which are notated herein as *Mandiani in Sénégal*. They are rarely played simultaneously in Guinea. The bell part as heard in Guinea is not as prominent throughout Sénégal. The drummers in Tambacounda used the bell or a substitute instrument most frequently. Over a period of six weeks I was able to return to Tambacounda and heard an ensemble comprised of predominantly young performers several times. By my last visit, a decision was made to leave out the bell part because it was confusing the dancers either because of the way it was played or simply because of the additional sound. In illustrations and performances of Mandiani in Dakar, Sénégal, the bell was not routinely used in casual settings but was heard in official performances.

According to Sénégalese dancer Oumoukaltom Diop, the important drum rhythm for dancing is played by the diun diun. "The djimbe plays solo, but I listen to the diun diun. The soloist plays with the dancer but the diun diun plays the rhythm to dance."

There is a single drum rhythm which is common in all three dances, Doundoumba, Mandiani, and Domba. This part is routinely played in Sénégal and Mali on the djimbe as illustrated in *Figure 2.21*. In Guinea, this rhythm was originally played on the sangbé or kenkeni. According to M'Bemba Bangoura, one of the directors of the Guinea National Ballet determined that this part would be better if played on the djimbe.

In sessions with djimbe drummers from Sénégal and Guinea, two concepts prevailed toward the creation of parts. Generally among

Djimbe I

Figure 2.21
Accompanying Djimbe Rhythm common to
Doundoumba, Mandiani and Domba.

Sénégalese drummers, the parts are fixed. The Guinea drummers, on the other hand, have an approach which allows for the creation of multiple parts, one for each drummer. Gbanworo Keita, principle djimbe drummer with Les Ballets Africains, commented through translator Ricki Stein that "If you have many drummers, it is possible to create parts or reconfigure the existing parts to provide more variety among the players for any rhythm." In established ensembles, the lead djimbe player makes those decisions.

Drummers

"A good player is known for the variety of rhythms he plays. An excellent drummer is known for his improvisations." (Drame 1979)

The lead drummer has two principal functions. The first role is that of musical director. If the musicians are playing in a purely musical context, without dancers, the lead player will signal the beginnings, endings and indicate phrase segments of the selected rhythms. The lead player is the designated soloist unless that function is temporarily granted to another player. Within each Mande community there is generally one player affirmed by the community to this position. My observations in Sénégal suggest that there is also a commonly accepted order of succession to the positions should the affirmed lead player not be present.

The second responsibility of the soloist or lead player is to accompany the dance. Solo improvisations are intended to amplify or enhance movements executed by the dancers. When asked how a lead player thinks of solo playing in Mandiani, Abdou Kounta and Mor Thiam both responded, "When playing Mandiani, you play Mandiani solos." The understanding here is that the drummer's solos will be shaped by the character of the movements, the expertise of the dancers, as well as the creativity of the drummer. It is possible for the dancer, within his or her own creative efforts, to inspire the drummer who in turn creates musical phrases accordingly. It is also possible for the drummer to propel the dancer into creating movements not considered in the past.

The solo language is either derived from the dance movements, commonly practiced rhythmic cells, or from culturally recognized rhythm patterns. Many of these rhythm patterns can be heard in the spoken language of the people. During a conversation with Mor Thiam, he said that in some instances while playing music "the drum speaks

Translation: *Gna nu mom*
                Bungnuy dundaak, bungnuy dé yep
                Gna nu   mom Sama.

Figure 2.22
A Familiar Phrase Playable on a Variety of Drums.

the language." With that comment, he spoke a phrase and then played the same phrase on his djimbe. "If the drummer is playing and someone walks in, he (the drummer) can tell you who the person is and what this person has been doing" (with phrases played on the djimbe.) In many African languages, there are phrases and proverbs which are spoken regularly, and they are recognizable as sound patterns even when the words are not articulated. These sound patterns can be reproduced on a variety of instruments including the djimbe. The phrase in *Figure 2.22* was heard during a 1989 political rally in Kaolack, Sénégal as the favored local candidate arrived. The variation in *Figure 2.23* was offered by Konte. According to Konte, this particular proverb relates to the

Translation: *Gna nu mom, Kujamaat sama hel dem thi gath*
                Bungnuy dundaak, bungnuy dé yep
                Gna nu mom Sama.

Figure 2.23
A Familiar Phrase Variation.

strong belief held by the Wolof speaking people of Sénégal in the power of the ocean spirit. In a performance of the opening phrase, the context will clarify the application. The proverb, translated by Madiguene Seck, says, "A man was bitten by a snake, and as the man lay there between life and death, he spoke, saying, 'Whether we are alive or dead you still own us.' " Sénégalese actor/dancer Thierno N'Diaye Dit Doss translated this phrase as it was used by saying, "It means, you are our boss, whether we are alive or dead, you are our boss."

Stylistic elements common to solos played by most djimbe players include the following: 1) short phrases, usually one to three seconds in duration; 2) hemiola to extend a melodic idea; and 3) the 2:3, 3:4 relationship between the solo and accompanying material. *Figure 2.24* is an example of djimbe solo material using 2:3 and 3:4 relationships, repetition and the reconfiguration of rhythmic ideas, that is, four sixteenth note figures presented in duple meter, and four note groupings played in triple meter.

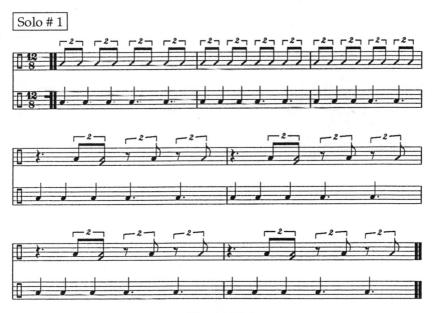

Figure 2.24
Djimbe Solo Examples with Diun Diun Accompaniment.

Solo # 2

Solo # 3

Figure 2.24, *continued.*

Solo # 4

Solo # 5

Figure 2.24, continued.

Solo # 6

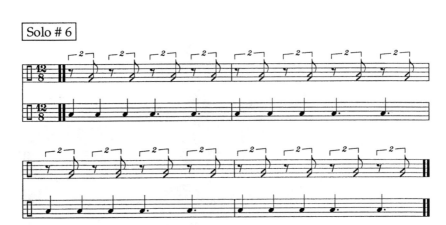

Solo # 7

Figure 2.24, *continued.*

Figure 2.24, continued.

***Figure* 2.24,** *continued.*

Figure 2.25
A Child Carried on a Mother's Back.

The Learning Process

Learning traditional music and dance is much the same all over Africa. Ghanaian dancer/drummer C. K. Ganyo said, "I started learning the rhythms in the womb and the dances on my mother's back." If one can agree with the concept of prenatal learning, this statement is completely accurate. In most African societies, both traditional and contemporary, infants are rarely far from their mother or a responsible female. The child is often securely wrapped and carried on the female's back while she performs many of her daily tasks. An example of this very typical arrangement is shown in *Figure 2.25*. This is not an unusual scene in the market place or at many social events. Mondet and Drame observed that children carried in this way "are basically unaffected by all the activity and still sleep if they want."[13] I also observed a woman in Ziguinchor, Sénégal who appeared to be about seven months pregnant dancing quite vigorously with no problems at all.

Through the years many authors have discussed the method of learning followed by the majority of African drummers. Young drummers observe older experienced players to acquire the techniques of tone production and style. If there are experienced drummers in their own age group, the more experienced player may offer suggestions. Generally, novice musicians are left to their own devices to develop technically. I observed several young musicians from a youth group formed in Dakar, Sénégal, who were learning in this fashion. Two very young boys, four or five years old, were heard drumming on Gorée Island. From a distance the sound of their drumming was excellent. When I rounded the corner and saw them, I was very surprised at the source. They were practicing on tin cooking oil cans and cardboard boxes.

In Bargny, a community about 30 kilometers from Dakar, I saw an clear example of the traditional learning process. In this community the Tabala drums are associated with Sufi drumming and the Khadir, one of three Moslem sects in Sénégal. Their religious meetings occur on Thursday evenings and drumming is a prominent part of this service. The drummers were all male but both men and women sang. In addition to the expected separation of women and children from the men in a public setting, there was a large group of boys seated directly behind and beside the drummers. Each seemed very intent on absorbing all of the drumming activity. Ten days later there was a celebration at one of the homes in the community. Before the start of the celebration, the same boys were drumming in the background. It was apparent that these young men were apprentices and preparing to assume these responsibilities in the future.

Costume

A costume can be defined as: "1) the prevailing fashion in coiffure, jewelry, and apparel of a period, country or class; 2) a suit or dress characteristic of a period, country, or class; and 3) a person's ensemble of outer garments . . ." In performance arts, costuming is rarely limited to articles of clothing.[14] For African music and dance these definitions are expanded to include anything worn or carried on the body during performance, and include the musical instruments used in the performance. By considering what is seen and heard we include objects such as theatrical "properties" or "props."

The fabric used for daily wear in West Africa, more so than many other regions of the continent, is strongly oriented to waxed prints and patterns, as well as western styles. In other parts of the continent, Kenya, Zaire, and South Africa for example, the daily wear is almost exclusively western or European in design. In the contemporary Moslem communities, the dress often reflects traditional Arabic styles for both men and women. Sénégal, Mali, and Guinea have a strong Moslem/Arabic presence. Christianity and western ideologies, brought to these areas during the colonial period, introduced European styled clothing which became a design standard. For example, clothing worn by women attending social events might reflect European high fashion designs made with recognizably African print fabric, or a traditional African ensemble, such as the grand boubou, ndoket, seurre, marinière or taillebasse and moussr (see *Figure 2.26)*. As one might expect, urban areas are much more western in their approach to dress than rural locations, possibly because of the non-agrarian lifestyle followed by city dwellers and the international awareness that comes with urban living through the print media, television, and films. In smaller towns and villages, one is much more likely to see clothing styles that suggest the historical past with less attention to western design and related ideas of high fashion.

The total number of layers and quantity of cloth worn by women is generally linked to the wearer's age group. In the traditional village, young girls before the age of puberty might only be required to use a single seurre, and often not required by custom to wear much else. Beyond puberty, a female might be expected to wear a form of upper and lower body covering consisting of a bouba and a single or double seurre which is acceptable at knee length or above. After marriage, women are expected to wear more modest covering. The seurre is often a two layered wrap. The under piece is generally a lighter weight fabric and often shorter than the one worn over it. The under seurre is generally a lighter color or white. Following child birth, women will often wear multiple seurres and an additional smaller piece of fabric used during the course of daily activity for many purposes such as carrying items home from the market, or it might be used to tie the baby to her back so that her hands are free to go about the business of the day (see *Figure 2. 25)*. Fifty years ago, it was the fashion to wear multiple seurres of graduated length, each being a different color or design.

The articles of clothing worn on the upper body in contemporary society are the marinière, taillebasse, or similar fitted tops often fashioned after turn of the century colonial French styles. The taillebasse is a fitted garment and the marinière a loosely tailored item. Past the normal stage of child bearing, a woman will wear a grand bouba, a large loosely hanging garment resembling a caftan. Although not typically seen in daily urban settings, in remote village environments, girls and

Grand Boubou, Moussr, Seurre

Taillebasse, Moussr, Seurre

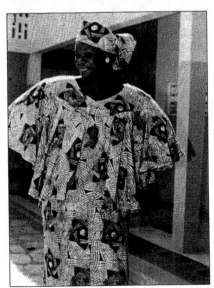

Marinière, Moussr, Seurre

Ndoket, Moussr, Seurre

Figure 2.26
Traditional Ensembles for Women.

possibly young unmarried women may not be pressed socially to wear tops at all. The possible alternative might be a bra alone or some other minimal garment resembling what might be called in the west a tube top. This may be nothing more than a band of fabric tied around the chest. As females mature, they may wear a panel covering the front of the chest and tied around the neck and lower back. This is often referred to as a halter top. After marriage, traditional clothing requirements are usually imposed.

There are several options for women performers suggested by Keba Diouf, costumer with the National Ballet of Sénégal, and others from Sénégal. Women can wear a short seurre decorated with pom-pons (originally made of Lambs wool, but now made of yarn) cowrie shells, and pearls. These seurres can be cut in such a way that a variety of designs result when they are wrapped. These panels may be made of fabric, animal skin, or bead work, and they may be of varying sizes, lengths and shapes. Women might also wear a headband, moussr or a small hat with a pointed top and horse hair rising from the point (hat not pictured). A cowrie shell covered bra is also standard performance attire. These options are pictured in *Figure 2.27.*

Another example of traditional clothing is the belefeté. There are many variations for this garment but in its most basic form, it is two mid-thigh length fabric panels attached at the waist and open at the sides. Performance clothing in any of these varieties is generously decorated with pom-pons and other dangling objects. Females in African performing groups might dance in the belefeté topless or wear a bra covered with cowrie shells.[15] With this ensemble, a headband or some other minimal head covering is used. With full dress options which cover the body more completely, the head is usually wrapped as well. An example of performance clothing for females is offered in *Figure 2.27.*

Men may wear typically Arabic dress as pictured in *Figure 2.28* such as the grand boubou, tourky or anango, sabador, farouk, thiayas, and daba. The grand bouba is essentially a large fabric panel. It is in the decorative stitching patterns and neck design where one differentiates between garments for men or for women. The sabador is a long, loose fitting garment with sleeves like a shirt. The tourky is a shorter version of this garment. The farouk is a simple fabric panel which covers the the chest and back. It is shoulder width and a bit longer than waist length. It is usually held secure with one or two straps on either side. Draw

Figure 2.27
Items Worn by Female Performers — Cowrie bra, seurre, moussr.

string or elastic straight legged pants called toubey, daba with a full lowered crotch, or thiayas with a full crotch lowered to mid-calf or below may be worn by male dancers. Musicians would perform in the same variety of clothing styles. Their choice is often dependent on the degree of mobility and local dress codes. Since there are no ritual or sacred connotations associated with Mandiani as it is currently performed, clothing worn is generally associated with social occasion.

In the semi-formal and staged versions of Mandiani performed by dance companies in Sénégal, Mali, and Guinea references have been made to specific costuming. Keba Diouf suggested that male dancers wear thiayas or raffia (grass skirt). It is acceptable now to wear raffia over short pants. A chest piece, or chest and back piece, in a variety of

Grand Boubou, Toubey

Sabador, Toubey, Mbahané

Tourky, Thiaya

Sabador, Toubey, Gris gris

Figure 2.28
Traditional Ensembles for Men.

shapes and sizes suspended from the neck or shoulders, and secured by two thin strings at the sides to limit shifting is regularly worn. These chest pieces are now often made of fabric and decorated with beads or cowrie shells. However, an older photograph of The National Ballet of Sénégal showed a male dancer wearing a chest piece made of animal skin. According to Diouf, arm bands worn on each arm, and headbands decorated with beads and cowrie shells can also be worn. The items worn by male performers are pictured in *Figure 2.29*.

The drummers, traditionally male, have very specific attire. The djimbe player can wear toubey, thiaya, or daba. Raffia may be worn, but it is usually seen without long pants. According to Diouf and Bangoura, drummers can wear raffia, however, current practices make raffia a principal costuming material for dancers. The drummers observed in the national performing companies, as well as those of regional and semi-professional status in Sénégal, Mali and Guinea did not consistently wear one style top or chest piece. Often times they wore no tops at all.

All djimbe players wore a hat. The hat is normally crescent shaped and positioned so that the curved shape rises six or more inches in the front and arches from the forehead to the base of the skull. The arc is extended with horse hair or similar material following the contour of the hat. The hat may also be decorated with cowrie shells, beads, or reflective disks usually made from mirrors or polished metal. Each of these items can be and often are used as fetishes. Marabous (a type of shaman) and fetishers in Sénégal explained that each item may have a purpose. The mirrors are intended to reflect any ill wishes directed toward the wearer back to their point of origin. An example is pictured in *Figure 2.30*. Other objects on the hat may carry prayers and medicines as various forms of protection.

Drummers and dancers have their own forms of protective fetishes and medicines. They are either worn in small pouches tied around the body, or carried in the form of bracelets, amulets, etc. During the classes I attended in Sénégal in 1987, 1989 and 1992, most of the arm bands and belts worn by our drum instructor were forms of protection. One drummer discussed the fetishes or gris gris he wore. Each had a specific application. One was to protect him when he traveled. Another was to protect him while playing drums. The system used for fastening another allowed him to adjust its powers to the situation. The most powerful one was given to him by his father and was for everything. There were a few costuming items given to the students in class for our

Mbahané, Thiaya, Chest piece

Farouk, Toubey

Chest piece, Raffia

Tourky, Grand Thiaya

Figure 2.29
Items Generally Worn by Male Performers.

Figure 2.30
Hat Worn by Djimbe Drummer.

final recital performance. Later the instructor commented that those things were just for "decoration."

The drum can also be decorated. On several occasions a piece of cloth was used to cover the exterior side of the djimbe bowl. The kesingkesings (metal plates) can be considered a form of decoration along with their musical function. Several of these sound enhancing devices were either etched or painted. In Sénégal, Guinea, and Mali the use of kesingkesings varies. The drummers of Guinea, according to M'-Bemba Bangoura, always use them. The djimbe players from Mali may not regularly use them. The Sénégalese drummers use these devices infrequently. In fact, in three out of four groups seen in Dakar, Sénégal, kesingkesings were used on the drum to achieve visual and sonic impact in performance but not for classes.

This chapter was designed to provide a body of information which frames Mandiani in the African context. In order to understand the components which reflect continuity between Mandiani in Africa and Mandiani in the United States the materials in Chapters Two and Three are presented in such a way that the reader can make immediate comparisons. Those elements which have changed through this continental transition will be those which reflect aesthetic concepts at work in the African-American community.

Chapter Three

Mandiani in
the United States:
A Discussion of Aesthetics

To attempt a description of the total Black aesthetic position for every issue confronting members of the Black diaspora would take a lifetime and more because these positions by nature change with each generation. Nonetheless, we can explore the music and dance culture associated with Mandiani and use this exploration as a window to examine related issues.

Mandiani provides a manifestation of Black aesthetics for African-Americans involved in the presentation of this music and dance form. Mandiani has been defined by a twentieth century generation of African-American performers and gives a clear reflection of their aesthetic beliefs. Chapters One and Two provided a general history of the dance in both Africa and America as well as a general description of Mandiani as it exists today in West Africa.

Performances of Mandiani by African-Americans are the result of individual interests, desires, and sometimes, their sense of responsibility. In Chapter Three we will examine the physical, psychological, and emotional qualities called upon by African-Americans to perform this dance. By doing so we will provide concrete data, defensible concepts, and definable processes used in the decision to learn and perform Mandiani. By utilizing the eyes, ears, hearts, and souls of those who have chosen to perform this music and dance, we will contribute to the understanding of a larger Black aesthetic.

How people understand and why they enjoy activities can be directly attributable to cultural aesthetics. In his discussion of "Universals in

Music," psychologist and ethnomusicologist Dane Harwood provided four basic concepts that I have adopted to look at the processing, understanding, and appreciation of Mandiani in the African-American community:

> First, a musical performance relates to prior performances. That is, performers and listeners have expectations about what is to happen. These expectations are based on experiences with other performances, other hearings in other contexts . . . A second source of musical meaning is the relationship of a particular performance to the way music is played and understood by the community in general. Third, a musical performance generates meaning in the relationship it has to the present audience, which may be performers as well as listeners. Finally, musical meaning accrues through contextual relationships other than those deriving from the audience.[1]

Aesthetic values and judgments regarding Mandiani in the African-American performance community also reflect concepts of continuity and change, that is, the process of making Mandiani one's own. The original rhythms or dance movements may be altered subtly in the transformation. These changes can be imperceptible to those adapting the music and dance to a new environment. In fact, the possibility is great that some change will occur. This process has been noted in the way Mandiani is played in Guinea, Sénégal, Mali, even before it was heard in the United States. Yet, the dance remains recognizably the same. These changes are easily understandable when one takes into account the individuality and creativity of performers. Even though a consensus defining Mandiani or what is acceptable as Mandiani within each group has developed, there is often a tolerance for variation during which innovation and creativity are realized. Individual interpretations have led to regional differences in the United States stemming from several African sources. These movement and music variations might be compared to regional dialects as found in linguistic studies. I have noted that these regional interpretations may vary to such a degree that rhythms or movements, although recognized, may not be fully understood or interpreted similarly by representatives from different regions. Accepting the foregone possibility, there are elements that remain consistent in the United States with African performance practices. These consistencies and/or slight variances can be useful in recognizing elements within the Black aesthetic.

African Music and Dance in the African-American Community

Song and Singing

On several occasions African musicians living in the United States were asked for songs that would be appropriate for Mandiani. The song provided in Chapter Two was familiar to many performing groups. Because singing in foreign languages can be problematic, not only to English speaking African-Americans but also to anyone singing a song in a language which is not their own, each group has a different pronunciation or variation on a similar lyric. The songs used do not feature long verbal phrases which might require rapid and precise articulation.

African-Americans easily accept the notion that vocal music is an important part of many African cultures. An effort is made by most established performing groups to include as many songs as possible with the dances they perform. As part of a staged performance in Philadelphia for example, one performing ensemble used the national anthem of Guinea to preface the dance Mandiani. The songs used by African-Americans when presenting the music of Africans generally contain short verbal phrases. The songs are sung before the dancing begins and they are often presented without percussion accompaniment. The songs are sung as call and response. Song texts suggested by many performers for Mandiani are related to celebrations of one form or another and often suggest an agricultural event.

Stylistic approaches to singing are quite prominent in African-American vocal culture. The variety of techniques used in producing vocal sounds are quite extensive and they are heard in singing styles such as the Blues, Jazz, and Popular music. Melisma or vocal slides, growl-like tones, and manipulating the pitch up and down are common approaches used by African-Americans. However, in singing African songs, this range of possible vocal techniques is not exploited. In fact, singers are often counseled not to use these vocal techniques. In the music heard on recordings and during live performances by African-Americans, the expectation is that the singers will use a clear, unaffected vocal style. There is a strong tendency to harmonize melodies using tonic, sub-dominant, and dominant chord structures as experienced in western harmonic traditions. These sounds are often reminiscent of harmonies heard in the Black church. Singers are also counseled not to harmonize.

Age and Occasion for Mandiani in the United States

Mandiani is neither age nor gender specific to African-American performers. Drum and dance classes provide the exposure to African performing arts for most African-Americans. These classes are frequently divided into three groups: children, teenagers, and adults. Rarely are there participants above the age of fifty in dance classes even though elders of the Mande cultures regularly participate as musicians and dancers. Each age group has its own motivation for involvement with Mandiani drum and dance.

Very young children may be interested because dancing and drumming is highly charged. With this age group there is not an in-depth understanding of the cultural association between Africa and African-Americans. Teenagers involved in the the performance of Mandiani, on the other hand, have had time to begin to understand their cultural connection. They do often require external motivation to become involved with music and dance activity. This motivation often comes from parents who themselves are interested in or would like their children to have contact with African culture, particularly since it is unlikely that this contact will be made through public education. With the teenage population, there is also the possibility of peer association, the social element. Those who are interested in African music and dance will often entice their friends to become involved.

Young adults, age 18 to 30, are the least active in African music and dance activities except as a targeted population in specially funded projects. The idea of using these music and dance activities for recreation or education has not been shown to be important to this age group. The response from those in this age group is that there are many other activities directly related to higher education, becoming financially independent, and providing their own livelihood which require their full efforts. The energy required to pursue these primary activities relegates African music and dance to a very low priority. There is also a bit of embarrassment in the association with Africa and African culture that inhibits participation. Prior to the second half of the 20th century many African-Americans believed identifying with Africa in any way would have a negative impact on their social standing.

Individuals 30 and older can be divided into two distinct groups. The largest group of individuals involved with this activity is middle-aged, 30 to 45. This group has had time to establish themselves in the work force and develop a family. They have a stronger sense of community responsibility and greater control over their discretionary time. There is also a greater financial independence for many which allows them to follow leisure interests rather than mandatory obligations. Individuals 50 and older, if they have not been involved with athletic activities throughout their life, are not anxious to start with African music and dance. They are, however, the most supportive age group through community activities and for children, either as interested family members or community members at large. It is generally accepted that Mandiani may be danced by men and women.

In the United States, the ratio of women to men involved as dancers is conservatively estimated at three or four to one, sometimes with no men at all. Drummers and drum classes, on the other hand, are usually all male. There are exceptions. A few professional performing ensembles do have female drummers. These women typically play the diun diun, however, there are two female djimbe players I am aware of in the United States who function as lead drummers. Female djimbe players can also be observed occasionally playing supporting drum parts for dance classes.

Dance companies which perform Mandiani are a relatively new phenomenon. Historically, there were celebrations among African-Americans which may have included African styled dance such as the gatherings in Congo Square in New Orleans; 'Lection Day' when it was celebrated during the mid-1700s; John Conny Festivals; and Pinkster celebrations of the antebellum period. These events have since faded from the social calendar. Contemporary events in the African-American community include Juneteenth and Kwanzaa. These celebrations often take place in an atmosphere which welcomes African music and dance. Although music and dance activities are often planned for these celebrations, they are rarely intended to highlight a specific African culture. Therefore, the occasions for which Mandiani is performed are generally attended by people who have experienced dance classes where Mandiani has been taught. In these instances, the performance venue can be an informal space, or a concert stage. The dance class and the concert performance will be discussed in the following passages for the drummer and the dancer.

The Drum and the Drummer

Until recently, djimbe carvers have resided only on the African continent. African-American drummers who have attempted to carve their own drums have been successful to a point, however, mass production was never their interest. Small wood workers have emerged as drum makers in the United States, but they usually serve a limited market. Recent efforts have been made to produce djimbes with contemporary technology in the United States and Japan by major percussion instrument manufacturers such as Latin Percussion. These instruments are usually designed and produced with non-traditional woods and tuning systems like those used on the conga drum, rather than the traditional lace tuning system. These mass produced instruments are used by professionals but thus far they have not found their way into the African music mainstream in the United States. Many African-Americans bound to traditional African culture preclude the use of instruments that do not carry with them the mystique of Africa. These contemporary products do carry a promise of predictability and stability for professional players. A drum from Africa may not be as important to the drummer when that person attempts to make their own drum. In that instance the drum becomes important as a personal creation.

Sound and Frequency Range

As we consider the levels for music volume and frequency range during leisure times, two descriptions immediately come to mind: for many African-Americans, the music is loud, and the electronic equipment playing the music is adjusted so that the bass and other percussive sounds dominate. Mid-range adjustments are generally used to achieve the same results in vocal music. High decibel levels are part of the life-style for many African-Americans.

While discussing volume and music listening habits with teenage dancers and drummers, they explained that high volume is required to hear "inside" the music, or, to hear all parts of the music. The research of Marie-Louise Barrenas and Fredrik Lindgrin, published in 1990, offers an explanation. Their research links noise tolerance to the degree of melanin[2] present in the inner ear and cochlea. These researchers cite work as early as 1931 on the "hearing function in coloured and white American hospital patients with the same cultural background." It was found that "hearing thresholds were superior in couloured (males) compared with white males in the frequency range above 2 kHz, and this difference increased with age." Their findings support the hypothesis that "individuals with high melanin content in the stria vascularis (a part of the inner ear) have more pronounced protection against noise exposure." Based on their research we believe that there is a biological basis for high noise tolerance that is transmitted from generation to generation in the African-American population based on the presence of melanin.

Drummers tend to evaluate a djimbe in three ways. The first consideration is based on the slap sound.[3] This is not an easy sound to achieve on every drum, and the ability to do so is often related to the diameter of the drumhead and the size of the player's hands. If you have small hands, the drumhead diameter does not have to be very large to achieve the sound without too much effort. Larger hands require larger head diameters. The average drum found in the United State has a head diameter of approximately thirteen inches. Larger and smaller instruments can be found, depending on the orientation of the player and instrument availablity. There are perceivable frequency differences in the resultant sounds. The highest overtones used to produce a dynamic slap are most easily activated near the edge of the drum. This slap sound comprises a major portion of improvised solo playing in the ensemble.

The second sound most often considered in the assessing the quality of a drum is the bass tone. The drumming habits of African-American djimbe players do not feature the bass sound extensively in improvisations and solos. The absence of frequent bass sounds in solo playing is a curious phenomenon because the listening habits in many African-American communities and the evaluation of the drum focuses on the bass sound. The third sound considered in the assessment of a drum is called the "tone."[4] This sound is not difficult to achieve and offers a contrasting timbre to the slap but is used sparingly by African-Americans for solo playing.

The diun diun may effectively provide sounds in the bass frequency range. Regardless of its overall size, the preferred tuning of the diun diun places its sound in the lowest acceptable range.[5] If there are two diun diun drummers, the general procedure is to have both diun diun drums play in unison. Although most African-American diun diun players are aware of the bell attached to the instrument as it is played in Guinea, not everyone uses the bell consistently. Abdoulai Aziz Ahmed cited a diun diun player in New York, Spanky, as one who has specialized in playing the diun diun for many years and is consistent with his bell playing. I have asked other diun diun players about bell parts. In many instances the player does not know the part. African-American drummers who have dedicated their efforts toward diun diun playing are rare. As a result, one might gather that the diun diun is the least desirable drum to play. Perceived reasons for this lack of interest will be discussed later in this section. Several classes I observed met with all participating drummers playing djimbe. In this instance, according to Bradley Simmons, one of the djimbe players would be assigned to play the diun diun part on the djimbe.

In my conversation with dancer/director Melvin Deal, he continually used the term "bombastic" while discussing the movements and music for Mandiani. He was referring to the fast tempo and high decibel levels. We have a general understanding of volume preferences through the young participants involved from the African-American community. In impromptu drumming sessions heard in New York, Pittsburgh, Philadelphia, and Phoenix when a variety of hand drums were present, the dynamic potential of the djimbe was clearly greater than that of the conga drum and in skilled hands it could easily dominate the sessions. Even in small djimbe ensembles, one or two drummers can create a considerable amount of sound. When four or five djimbe drummers are present, the volume level can be high enough to overpower any other thoughts, according to many of the dancers interviewed. Assane Konte articulated this sentiment when he said, "When all the drums are going right, it carries you to a higher level." Regardless of how one might choose to view these opinions, high decibel levels and the ability to play with high velocity are usually associated with power and being in command in the drum and dance ensembles. Put simply, sound is power.

A concern of some ensembles is the volume imbalance between lead and accompanying parts. Each drum has the potential to sound very loud; however, restraint should be used by those playing parts in order to remain at a dynamic level below the soloist. Regardless of the number of drums present, there remains an expected dynamic level which all players try to achieve. Konte also referred to the drums as being "hot."[6] In that statement, "hot" expressed the notion of well synchronized rhythms at high dynamic levels. For many, the concept of excitement is linked to volume alone. To general audiences, excitement and volume are almost inseparable, whereas synchronized movement and rhythms may not always register equally. For dancers and drummers synchronization of movement and rhythm, high energy and dynamic levels must all work together. The potential for physical damage to drummers and dancers exists while performing at such high speeds and volumes but this danger is often overshadowed by the desire to produce that level of excitement.

Beat and Rhythm

"Beat" is the term used to generally describe rhythmic qualities in music but there are a variety of specific elements implied. Beat is used by many to refer to pulse, tempo, syncopation, and accompaniment rhythms primarily heard in the bass and percussion instruments. Each has relevance as we discuss Mandiani, and each can be used to identify or at least qualify portions of the dance. Rhythm patterns have long been used in African and African-American culture to identify music and dance forms. Dance styles such as swing, disco, funk, and rap in the United States have specific rhythm patterns instantly associated with them. When a rhythm pattern is used to identify a particular dance form, there is often a range of acceptable tempi which allow the dance to retain its character. The drums which provide the fundamental low frequencies can produce a variety of complex rhythms which form the primary beats. Higher pitched drums provide additional variety. African-American music usually requires the rhythmic integration of all bass instruments, for example, the electric bass guitar, the bass drum, and the tom toms of the trap set in popular music. However, this approach to complex and highly integrated bass rhythms does not generally occur in Mandiani. African-American groups generally do not use multiple diun diun parts even if there are two or more players present with an instrument.

Each of the three dances discussed in Chapter Two has a very clear orientation toward triplet based rhythms. The majority of popular music in the second half of the twentieth century in the United States has had a tendency toward duplet interpretation. Mandiani's rhythmic background is distinctly a triplet pattern. African-Americans learning Mandiani have to assimilate a triplet orientated dance with their background which is strongly biased toward duplet rhythms. During the 1950s the existence of jazz, particularly the various forms of swing and bebop, were helpful in interpreting triplet based rhythm. For young drummers entering this music form, the interpretation of the diun diun part and the distinction between duplet and triplet based rhythms appears to be somewhat problematic. There are diun diun drummers who tend to reinterpret the triplet rhythm. A similar reinterpretation occurred in Latin America as the clave rhythm developed. *Figure 3.1* shows comparative examples for both of these reinterpreted rhythms from triple to duple meter.

This discrepancy and reinterpretation in djimbe solo drumming does not seem to present the same problem to djimbe drummers. The soloist often moves freely between duple and triple meter. The precedent for this rhythmic flexibility has been established in African-American music culture for a very long time. Jazz soloists cultivated this ability over eighty years ago. Through each period of its development, jazz interpretations varied and the distinction between triplet and duplet rhythm was blurred. Swing, bebop, cool, and fusion all required interpretive value judgements. Current popular dance music rarely utilizes triplet note values and "fusion jazz" has moved into the popular realm.

Health, Posture and Comfort

In our research three areas of concern were stressed by drummers. First, physical conditions that result from playing the drum; second, the traditional posture used for playing djimbe; and third, positions which are comfortable or provide relief when playing the djimbe for extended periods. Drummers often sacrifice comfort and healthful postures for

Figure 3.1
Reinterpreted Rhythms from Triple to Duple Meter.

playing positions that can add to the excitement and popular appeal in a performance.

Blood passed through the urinary tract is a condition known as hemoglobinurian (blood in the urine). Some players believe this condition results from carrying the drum strapped around the waist. One of the African drummers believed that intense playing purged the body of "bad" blood and this was a good thing. He was concerned that there was something lacking in the performance when the condition did not occur. In a newsletter entitled "The Talking Drum," Dr. Ernest L. Washington wrote that hemoglobinurian is a possibility for both dancers and drummers (1989, 19-20). This condition results from trauma to the red blood cells in the drummer's hands and the dancer's feet. These damaged red blood cells are filtered out of the blood by the kidneys and cause discoloration of the urine for a brief period. To minimize the ill effects on the kidneys, Dr. Washington suggests that artists drink a few glasses of water before beginning an activity. The strap around the drummer's waist has very little to do with the condition.

When playing accompaniment, the common posture for djimbe players in the United States and Africa is standing upright. This is a posture used when the drum is strapped to the player's waist or carried by straps over the shoulders (see *Figure 2.16*). Carrying the drum strapped around the waist is comfortable because the weight of the drum is supported low on the body by the pelvis, however, this carrying method was used by a relatively small number of players. Drummers expressed concern that the strap may exert unusual pressure on the kidneys and may cause damage to the organ.

The posture used by djimbe soloists has several symbolic interpretations but there may also be sound physical justification. The use of the legs in lifting heavy objects is promoted by physical trainers and medical personnel as the safest way to lift heavy objects. In describing how a person should lift heavy objects, or in weight training how to execute one form of the exercise known as a "dead lift" or "squat," trainers and doctors have determined that the bent knee and arched back posture is the safest way possible. The djimbe and the diun diun may weigh between twelve and thirty pounds, depending on their size and the materials used for their construction. Over a long period of time and after constant pressure from downward blows, these drums can feel very heavy. By wearing the straps over the shoulders the weight of the drum is equally distributed on both sides of the body.

When standing erect and upright, this carrying system may present minor difficulties for the drummer in either holding the shoulders back or standing completely erect. For djimbe soloists, wearing the straps over the shoulders seems to be a very effective carrying system, particularly if the player intends to assume the soloist's posture we discussed earlier. As that posture is assumed, it is also very important to engage the muscles used to arch the back, along with keeping the chest open. When standing this way, the spine is in its strongest position. The over the shoulder carrying system also facilitates resting the drum completely on the ground or floor. With the drum resting on the ground, the drummer is free to focus all energies on playing the instrument.

Any change from a static playing position is welcomed by drummers. Soloists achieve intensely dramatic visual effect by rolling over on their backs and supporting the weight of the drum with their knees and shins while playing. It is not an easy position to assume gracefully, which may explain why this position is used infrequently. When it is employed, however, audiences are quite thrilled even though the actual music played from this position may, out of necessity, be rather simplistic. The kneeling positions described earlier also provide relief from the weight of the drum and add theatrical interest as well. When playing in a stationary position, drummers rarely carry the drum to their side because the drumhead rests at an awkward angle for dramatic or articulate playing. While walking, this carriage is commonly used because leg movements are uninhibited by the drum.

Part of the attraction to hand drumming is that the player has direct physical contact with the drum. There is no distance or physical apparatus between the performer, the instrument and the sound produced. Part of the satisfaction in playing a drum is derived from successfully developing the technique required to produce the appropriate sounds on demand. When the djimbe is struck, there is added pressure to the shoulders or waist depending on the system used to suspend the drum. The player also feels the impact on the legs where the drum rests. This completed cycle of contact and the body's physical response to the blow creates a completely personal experience between the drummer and the drum.

Calluses often develop on the drummer's hands either from the constant trauma due to impact or from the constant rubbing of the diun diun stick on the side of the hand. These calluses at the edge of the palm and on the fingers of djimbe players affect the instrument's sound in a

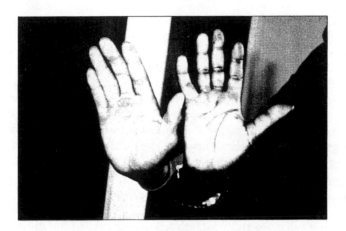

Figure 3.2
Calluses Developed from Playing the Djimbe.

positive way by providing a harder, smaller contact point when the hand strikes the drumhead. *Figure 3.2* shows the right hands of two different drummers and typical calluses. The callus is a point of pride with many players. In gatherings of veteran players and new initiates, calluses are sometimes brandished as symbols of established performers. There are a few recognized djimbe drummers who do not display typical callous build-up on their hands. There is a mystique surrounding these players. I asked how they are able to achieve their wonderful sounds without developing calluses. One well known drummer without calluses smiled at the question but was not willing to respond. The implication given was that good technique does not depend on calluses.

Understanding Solo Concepts

There are examples in African music where music funtions as a language. We asked African born drummers to explain how their concept of solo or lead playing was developed. For them, solo playing involves concepts in both music and language. Djimbe hand drumming shares basic musical elements with the conga drum. Both musics have "parts" which come together to create a basic rhythmic matrix. There are, however, differences in their sonic structure. Music from the Caribbean and Latin America had existed in the United States well before the 20th century. The principal Latin-American hand drumming which emerged as a part of popular culture in the United States in the mid-1940s emanated from Cuba and the Yoruba or Lucumi music found there. In the accompaniment rhythms for cultural dances from Cuba, there is an undeniable emphasis on tonal contour. A collection of two or three conga drums can create an accompanying "melody" which provides the basic pattern over which the soloist improvises. In the accompaniment, one note flows into another or is dependent on another to complete this melodic shape. The soloist is free to integrate solo sound into that accompaniment or create a rhythmic variation apart from it.

In Mande cultures, an emphasis on tonal shape does not appear as significant. Even though parts are played on drums which are tuned to various pitch levels, that variance may be very small. In Guinea, the ensembles have many different parts that are played. To distinguish these parts, pitch variance from each drum is helpful but not always necessary for each part. In Sénégal, there are fewer parts played. (See *Figures 2.14, 2.15,* and *2.18*). In the Guinea ensembles the doun douns, kenkeni, and sangbé produce a melody-like phrase when all drums are present. The diun diun music of Sénégal and Mali is not as oriented to melody.[7]

Although there may be multiple drums used in each of these countries, the drum music seems to be constructed linearly, that is, each drum part is a complete musical idea or phrase unto itself. When these parts are combined, a rhythmic texture is created that does not permit the easy distinction of any one part, but a rhythm/sound matrix emerges that is greater than the sum of its rhythmic components. This compositional characteristic is very different from other African drum musics which rely more on tonal sequence or solos played along with other drums which respond.[8]

According to native djimbe drummers and well-respected African-American players, drumming in the Mande cultures, particularly solo drumming, draws its fundamental constructs from spoken language with a strong tendency for polyrhythmic applications of triplet over duplet rhythms and hemiola. Phrases in the soloist's musical language match the spoken language I heard by sounding in short phrases with acute accents. While listening to two Sénégalese women conversing in the Wolof language, it was intriguing to hear the rhythmic qualities in their conversation. They spoke at a speed which seemed to match the rate at which drum soloists generate solo material, and the words flowed at a tempo consistent with many dances, including Mandiani. The rhythm in their speech resulted primarily from alveolar (tongue-gum ridge) sounds like those associated with "d", "t" or "n"; palatal (tongue-hard palate) which is the rolled "r" sound; and velar (tongue-soft palate) as with the "g", "j", or "k" articulations. The consonant sounds of the Mande languages are also spoken quite percussively. The stop-plosive articulations created accents in the flow of sound as would the changes from "slap" to open "tone" create accents in djimbe playing. In order to speak drum rhythms the vocables used to initiate articulation are generally bilabial using both lips to create sounds like "ma", "b" or "p."[9]

Another equally important factor in generating solo ideas is the visual representation of rhythms created by the dancers. The solo dancer, as is often the case, will enter the dance arena, perform for a brief period, then return to the larger group of dancers. The djimbe sound is expected to accent the dancer's movements and provide a rhythmic interpretation or enhancement of the dance variations being performed. These accents are expected by the audience and other performers in the development of solo passages with or without dance. Drummer Usef Manne, a drummer we visited in Kafountine, Sénégal, explained that when the dancer presents a movement, it is the drummer's responsibility to say what this dancer is doing.

Several ideas from cognitive psychology may be useful in explaining the development of solo material produced by djimbe players in Africa and the United States. In 1968, Simon and Sumner presented several basic premises which influenced the then developing theory on music coding and the construction of melodic and harmonic sequences. "Intuitively, the construction of melodic and harmonic sequences seem to be rule governed."[10] This process may also be true for solos developed by djimbe players. Working through intuition is the standard for solo drumming. Rules for solo development are implied but not stated. There are culture-based procedures for listeners and performers, therefore, rules must also exist governing these procedures.

Mandiani music contains culturally recognized rhythmic and pitch components, along with a multi-layered pattern structure which is part of Mande performance practice. There must be rules, although intuitive ones, which regulate solo development. By examining each of these premises, the relationship between the development of solos along with the drummer's concept of melodic and harmonic sequences in the djimbe ensemble may be understood. The premises suggested by Simon and Sumner are:

①*The listener develops expectations for successive events.*

Procedures exist which regulate the succession of events for dance in Africa and the United States. The dance student in the United States requires that clear repeated rhythms mark or imitate the dance movement very closely. There is usually a set number of repetitions for each dance movement, and there is the expectation of certain musical cues to signal the changes from one movement to the next. This easily becomes routine with drummers and dancers who work together regularly.

Audiences have developed expectations concerning music sound, movement style, dance length, and the general character of the total performance in the concert hall and the village. Possibly the most important expectation of the African-American audience is that the music and dance will not remain the same for more than a few minutes. The cycle of repetition in African-American dance performance is relatively short when compared to typical African dance in the African context. In Africa, the dancer and drummer together will perform short segments even though the specific music and dance may last a very long time. The djimbe drummer, without a dancer to attend to, will often develop long phrases with rhythmic cells that are repeated many times, keeping in mind the primary process for musical development in Mande culture as well as many other African cultures is repetition. A repeated cell can create great tension and breaking away from the repeated figure becomes the release of tension. Also within this repeated cell, a careful process of variation can take place. The repetiton becomes familiar to the listener and subsequently, the variation becomes even more exciting. In the United States, the concept of change within a short period of time has a direct bearing on solo material developed. There are no expectations for long phrases and extended cycles of repetition as in African drumming. The use of extended repetition is, however, prevalent in various forms of popular music in the African-American community.

② *The rule operates on small well defined sets of elements.*

If the djimbe solo material is derived from the language of the people, a well defined set of elements will also include characteristics of spoken language. Focusing on African-American drummers, it is unlikely that these musicians speak African languages. Consequently, the elements used in solo development by these players are often from both English and African language rhythm concepts. In describing how they acquired or internalized their solo concept, several players said that initially, they heard live performances and recordings and copied rhythmic ideas. Later in processing this material, their conceptualization was expanded to include the various sounds which the drum was capable of producing. Finally, this array of sounds became the basis for melodic development in the solo.

In analyzing the general playing style of African-American djimbe players, rhythm recognition is prominent. The sound coveted by many players in selecting a drum in the United States is also the dominant sound used in solo development, a sharp, crisp, slap. Although this drum sound is recognized as the "solo" sound or the sound most frequently used while playing solos in the United States, the vocable used is "pac," "pat" or a close derivative. The use of the word "solo" for both the slap sound and the activity for which it is used underscores its importance among players in the United States. This suggests that the slap is the quintessential solo sound. Djimbe drummer Ahmed believes differently and says the most important sound is the "open tone" to contrast to the sharper pac sound. The pac and open tone sounds are clearly distinguishable and are heard as the primary sounds in djimbe solos.

The bass tone has a limited carrying distance. The optimum distance for bass tone audibility is relatively close to the drum; outside, this would suggest within fifty feet of the drum. But in an enclosed area with or without a roof, the bass tone can easily be heard at a greater distance. Although M'Bemba Bangoura declared the bass sound is very important to djimbe drumming, African-American players do not use it as a major component in their solo work.

African and African-American players use a cellular concept in solo development. These short, rhythmic cells are originally derived from the music created to mark or define the dancer's movements. Typically, drummers use short note groupings with an equivalent duration of space between the bursts, or they develop cyclical rhythms when creating solos when dancers are not present. If dancers are performing, the solo rhythms generally correspond to the movements of the dancer/soloist or the ensemble movement pattern. The expectation with many American ensembles is that each time a particular dance movement is performed, the corresponding solo rhythm will also be the same or similar. This practice may be traced to the dance class where the dancers are accustomed to a familiar rhythm repeated as they learn the movements. Each drummer may interpret a particular movement differently, but each interpretation must be understood by the dancers.

③ *The rule can be described using a small number of operators (such as "same" and "next").*

Procedurally, this is a simple matter. If the designated soloist is familiar with the dancer, there is also an understanding of what that dancer can or will do. Normally the choreographer establishes an order for events which will not vary drastically in staged performances. In this case, the expectation is that events will be the same as planned. Familiarity between drummers and dancers may allow for brief moments of innovation when the individuals are not totally consumed with pre-set directions. The same or similar rhythm pattern or interpretation from the djimbe player's library of rhythm patterns will often occur with each given dance movement. Dancers either have a pre-arranged dance sequence or a familiar succession of movements. The resultant solo drum music will be conceived and perceived with this rule in mind.

④ *The rule can be applied recursively, producing hierarchically organized patterns of sub-patterns.*

The solo rhythm patterns played by experienced drummers in the United States are modeled after their African counterparts. However, with less experienced players, the solo is often an extended series of accented notes derived from a constantly moving and usually alternating hand pattern usually found in conga drumming. Djimbe players do occasionally find themselves in a position where it is necessary to play continuously. This is very evident when there is only one djimbe drummer. In this situation the player usually plays assertively for solo distinction and at a moderate volume for an appropriate background sound.

Experienced players generally adopt the short cellular approach. These cells are basically one to two seconds in length. After listening to many drummers for a period of time, it becomes clear that the number of basic patterns used for soloing is generally limited to not more than five or six. Interesting solos are achieved by creating permutations of these basic rhythm patterns by changing drum sounds, manipulating the pattern in some way, chaining patterns together, or repeating a pattern multiple times.

Rhythm patterns frequently acquire regional characteristics. Ahmed asserts that he can identify regional characteristics associated with different parts of the United States. Also, he can name the teacher from whom a djimbe player derives his major influences by hearing the patterns played by the individual. Yacine Guéye made a similar comment in Sénégal. The basic material used in a solo will be derived from regional tastes, dominant or popular players from a particular region, and individual creativity.

Accompaniment and solo patterns seem to have evolved to a high degree in the playing styles of Guinea. Of the samples collected, the drum ensembles from Guinea have the highest number of parts generated for the Mandiani rhythm (see transcription of Mandiani from Guinea, *Figure 2.20*, Example C.2). This complex of parts also creates an exciting background for the featured soloist. Solo material can and is often generated from the accompanying drum parts. These parts can be linked together, displaced by one beat, played in succession, and interpreted by using a variety of expanded or diminished note values within the solo. Sources for these patterns can be varied and can come from a wide variety of sources. They may be derived from the dance steps themselves, a rhythmic counterpoint to the dance movement, and linguistic patterns as well as innovative patterns developed by the player.

⑤ *Musical patterns are multidimensional; patterns*
can exist simultaneously on a number of different levels
(metric, rhythmic, melodic . . .).

Metric variation accounts for a major portion of drumming. By linking various note groupings, repeating asymmetric phrases, or creating tonal exchanges between the soloist's rhythms and other drum parts present, the resultant solo can be thought of as organic, emerging from the existent sound matrix. Another alternative uses rhythms developed by the dancer during his or her solo. With this approach, the variety results from the additional creativity of the dancer. If the drummer is responsive to the dancer's movement, rhythmic variations can easily be derived from articulating or interpreting the dancer's gestures with appropriate drumming patterns.

Melodic ideas are derived in three ways. First, the soloist uses the variety of sounds which can be produced on the djimbe. In this instance, the player is thinking of pitch levels, rhythms and phrase length. A second approach is to play the same rhythm as one of the existing background parts. By doing so, the soloist draws attention to that particular voice in the drum texture and the related melodic line. The third procedure might be to add new accents to existing sounds in the accompanying rhythms. These new accents shift the listener's focus to a different sound combination and create a new "melody."

Figure 3.3
Mandiani as Played in the United States and Related Parts from Guinea.

Parts

There are three parts which may be used to identify the dance to be performed or its accompaniment. First, the solo. By itself this is not a very clear indicator of a dance. If one recognizes the rhythmic realization of a dance movement that is performed to a particular dance, then identifying that dance is possible. This kind of identification is most reliable

Figure 3.4 *The Diun Diun Rhythm for Domba in Sénégal and an Interpretation for Mandiani in the United States.*

Figure 3.5 *Principal and Second Accompaniment
used by African-Americans for Mandiani.*

with and among musicians who have worked together for extended periods. The second possibility is much more reliable in many instances. As mentioned in Chapter Two, the diun diun part serves as one of the defining components of the rhythm. Virtually all of the rhythms of the Mande cultures which are played with the djimbe and diun diun orchestration are identified by the diun diun rhythm. This is not necessarily true among African-American drummers and dancers. Many Americans interviewed admitted incomplete knowledge about the diun diun parts and identified dances through certain djimbe rhythms. The second part or collection of parts distinguishing one dance from another is in the accompanying djimbe rhythms. The possibility exists for utilizing one djimbe rhythm in multiple dances. A primary example is the rhythm identified as "pat ti pat" and its use in Mandiani, Domba, and Doundoumba. Third, there are other parts associated with dance accompaniment that may be fragmented to generate smaller rhythmic units. Also, multiple parts may be combined depending on the number of drummers present.

Mandiani as it is played in Guinea uses the largest number of instruments, and the highest variety in instrumental parts. Yet even in the seven djimbe parts offered by M'Bemba Bangoura in *Figure 3.3*, there are rhythms played by African-American drummers that are not easily recognized as belonging to the Guinea version of Mandiani. They can be analyzed as abstractions or composites of various Guinea djimbe parts. A possible explanation for this occurrence is that the parts were probably extrapolated from recorded rather than live performances. *Figure 3.3* presents two examples of Mandiani parts, one as they are played in the United States. Chart two shows the parts used in Guinea.

By reviewing the versions of the Mandiani diun diun parts played by many drummers in the United States, the distinction can easily be made as to their origin. In the ensembles I have heard from Sénégal,

Mali, and the United States, they used only one diun diun. This suggests that the Mandiani played in the United States is modeled after examples from Sénégal or Mali.

The rhythm known as Mandiani in Guinea is sometimes identified as Domba in Sénégal, depending on the tempo. The discrepancy is rooted in the interpretation of the rhythms for these two dances. There is one interpretation of the Mandiani diun diun rhythm which is generally recognized in the United States. This interpretation was identified by Bayo as the Domba rhythm. *Figure 3.4* shows the diun diun part for Domba in Sénégal and how this rhythm is played in the United States for Mandiani.

With the exception of those djimbe players who have recently been associating with drummers from Guinea, there are three basic parts identified by African-American djimbe players as belonging to Mandiani. *Figure 3.5* illustrates the principal accompaniment part (A) and its variation (B), which is the displacement of the "pat ti pat" part by two eighth notes, and the third accompanying part (C), which are used by African-Americans. According to Bayo, part "C" belongs to the dance Domba, however, this is one of the first rhythm parts played by African-Americans for Mandiani. Two possible explanations for the limited number of parts used by African-Americans might be either the origin of the dance at the time they were brought to this country, or the number of djimbe drummers regularly in place for classes, ensemble, rehearsals, and performances. Three djimbe players can be expected at any event in the United States. Even in places where there are more drummers available, normally only three different parts are played. These three parts are doubled by any number of players beyond the basic three. The distribution of parts is based purely on the sound matrix that participants expect to hear. This available number of players may also result from other factors. The underlying reason for the relatively consistent low number of participant drummers may rest in the unwillingness of African-American drummers to play parts and accept the idea of being a background player.

The Social Element

The Dance Class

Drummers are generally present in less than half of the time period for dance classes. Warm-up time is used by the drummers to prepare their instruments. On-the-spot tuning usually involves placing the drum near a strong heat source or putting a few more twists in the lace system to tighten the skin. One contemporary philosophy followed by a group of drummers in the United States dictates that no heat be used to tighten the drum. This being the case, these drummers must tighten the instrument manually. This process usually happens outside of the rehearsal space. By doing so, less time is required for instrument preparation during the class. The time utilized for drum preparation is often an opportunity for drummers to interact socially, or for the lead drummer to assign parts to be played by the other drummers. The lead drummer is hired or requested by the dance teacher to serve in this capacity. Additional musicians may or may not be engaged by the dance instructor to play for the class. No formal invitation is issued to additional drummers. They are usually permitted to play but this is always at the discretion of the lead drummer.

The musicians are sometimes placed at the side, rather than in front of or behind the class, but usually in a position facing the class. The class generally progresses from one end of the space to another while executing movements. In this setting, the lead drummer is responsible for playing the signals which command the dancers to begin, change steps, and/or stop. It is also the lead drummer's responsibility to direct the other musicians. The class often ends with a review of all steps taught during the session. It is during this final closing period that all dancers are given the opportunity to perform a solo movement in the context of the material just learned. These solos are performed near or facing the drummers. As the last music is played, the dancers usually offer a gesture of gratitude in the form of a bow, or kneeling in front of the drummers, or a modified bow and tapping the floor with open palms and speaking the word "ashé."[11] to the performing musicians. At this time, the musicians are provided an opportunity to give way to highly intense playing with improvisation, and the classes end.

The Performance

A concert performance, whether it is formal or informal, is more than just music and dance. Taken in its totality, it is viewed as an event, usually undertaken by a group of people who have rehearsed together, who have designated roles in the organization, and who constitute a semi-professional or professional group. The venues for performance vary from full proscenium stages to open air community performance sites. The seating arrangement for those attending a performance is usually in front of a stage or staging area, maintaining some distance between the performers and the audience, but oriented in one direction. The performance is almost always executed in line or block orientation. The drummers are normally positioned to the side of or behind the dancers. The lead drummer is the only musician who is given latitude to move away from the normally static position usually at the rear of the staging area. During a performance the lead player has the responsibility both to interact with solo dancers and to direct the music through various coded signals, either verbal, kinetic or drummed. Customarily, the drummers are featured as part of the performance and assume a position center stage. Depending on the number of drummers available, the role of lead player may shift from the leader to another djimbe player at the leader's discretion, but rarely is this role shifted to the diun diun player when dancers are involved.

The Drum Ensemble

The hierarchy and political structure of the drum ensemble is defined and determined by playing ability, understanding the rhythms and parts, as well as understanding non-music issues related to the performance of African music. There is great competition among drummers, albeit tacit or restrained much of the time, for the position of lead player in the United States. Because of this observation, drummers playing one of the dance classes in New York were asked to explain the significance attached to playing lead. One prominent idea presented was that the lead player holds the most prestige. The attention is usually focused on this individual, but more importantly, the lead player is provided the greatest latitude to play variations or to deviate from prescribed parts. When playing lead, the individual is not usually required to play repetitive patterns. The hierarchy in the drum ensemble dictates that the lead player controls the music ensemble. The position of leader always falls to a djimbe player. Among most players, it is the desired position to hold. From this position, the lead player exerts a great deal of control over the proceedings in class and in performances.

Another rationale offered by several dance teachers suggests that drummers, usually male, often become involved with dance classes for the association with dancers, typically female. The perception of male dominated African societies, and the image of a male as lead drummer, and having control over the dance and dancers, represents a very popular concept among African-Americans. Often, this scenario is followed in the American ensemble. There is a minimal awareness or understanding of female directed or matriarchal societies in Africa. In the relationship between lead drummer and lead dancer, there must be a shared control to a certain degree in order to maintain the effective presentation of the music and dance. Among loosely organized drum groups, there are still competitive efforts to secure the position of lead player. On a few occasions, this competition for soloist status has led to physical confrontations between players.

Playing repetitive parts presents a personal challenge to many African-American drummers. Most of the musicians involved with djimbe drumming started by playing conga drums. In ensembles using the conga, even though there are specific parts to be played, the typical ensemble applications are jazz and popular music where playing variations on the rhythms is welcomed. Many of the players who first discovered the djimbe were also players in professional or recreational drumming groups where the role of lead player might be passed from one player to another. For some drummers, it is only after they have played in the djimbe ensemble for an extended period that the importance of stable part playing is realized.

There are many gratifications associated with playing hand drums. They may stem simply from physical involvement, which was the reason offered by most dancers and drummers. Satisfying the emotional or mental being was not brought up regularly during interviews after dance classes, but it was evident in the tone of these discussions. African-American drummers in the classes I attended in Sénégal and the United States were not as overtly social in their gathering and often required a period of time to define their individual roles in the ensemble. Identifying and conforming to an ensemble concept was not an easy adjustment for many players. In other music groups such as jazz and popular dance music ensembles, the drummer normally functions as the only percussionist in the ensemble, often enjoying wide latitude in creative and artistic behavior. Adhering to the restrictions required to perform African music was difficult for many drummers. Their previous musical experiences did not always prepare them for this demanding ensemble experience. Ego can be detrimental in any ensemble. Drummers who develop the ability to separate themselves from other external attitudes and pressures do well in developing the cohesiveness required to effectively produce djimbe music.

Evidence of friction between players in the United States was found in the reactions exhibited by many players performing as ensemble members rather than soloists. Many were attempting to match or exceed the dynamic level of the lead drummer or soloist. It was not always clear why these efforts were made. Performing at high decibel and intensity levels does tend to mask nonperformance related emotions and/or concerns. It also provides a non-verbal platform to strive for superiority. Challenges of this nature rarely result in good ensemble playing. If the drum ensemble can achieve proper balance in music and personality, functioning in an environment of personal commitment and human interaction can be a very satisfying experience.

Many drummers are involved in drumming activity because of its physical nature. The conditions which exist during periods of high physical demands can bring physiological gratification. For instance, after sustained levels of high exertion while performing, changes in the blood cause endorphins (a certain protein) to be released in the brain which elevate mood and affect one's attitude in such a manner that a calming effect results. Even moderate exercise has been recognized as an activity that relieves tension and anxiety. Hand drumming, especially djimbe playing, is capable of producing this physical state. The aspects of physical effort and related machismo gratification may be major contributors to popular trends which use drumming as a form of physical or psychological therapy. It may also explain the adoption of drumming by individuals involved in the men's movement which began in the mid-80s. Several drummers commented that the most satisfying characteristic of the djimbe is the act of wearing the drum when playing. In doing so, the drummer has a feeling of being at one with the instrument and the music as it is produced. This is not always the feeling one gets from playing the conga drum as practiced in the United States. In most instances, the conga drum sits on the floor or in a stand, and it is physically detached from the player. The fact that the djimbe is carried between the legs may also have further psycho-sexual implications.

Gender Issues

In the folkloric traditions practiced through music and dance, there is a universal relationship between men and women that has existed for centuries. In West African folk cultures women are rarely instrumentalists. They are more often singers and dancers. Female societies may provide their own music possibly using female musicians, however, the norm is to hire community or professional musicians who are most often male. Social music is not necessarily gender specific but the music provided for these events is typically provided by males.

In contemporary society, particularly in the United States, there is a clear movement toward equality of the sexes. Women's rights legislation is creating environments in the business and corporate world that support the equal treatment of men and women in the work place. Pressures for equality have emerged in the social fabric of society. The growing acceptance of gender equality is creating a recreation and leisure time environment which encourages women to participate in many formerly male dominated activities. Many of the professional African dance companies in the United States, and most of the semi-professional and community groups are directed by female dancers. Several of these ensembles are co-directed by male drummers. There are a few exceptions to the female dancer/leader profile such as the ensembles directed by male dancers Chuck Davis, Melvin Deal, and Assane Konte. Nonetheless, the directors are usually dancers.

Many people still regard African culture as "primitive" and because of this perception, these individuals look to African culture for traditional male and female role models. To this end, many males in the United States, regardless of ethnic background, have embraced drumming and African music as symbolic of the traditional male. Many believe that the equality pursued in western culture between men and women does not transcend these culture boundaries and that African traditions will support their concept of the male/female relationship. International touring companies often have women drumming at various times in a performance. Female drummers would usually be seen in a support role, placing the male drummers in the forefront. Images from routine daily life which show females drumming are rarely if ever seen by African-Americans. Ethnomusicologist Kwabena Nketia explained how individuals might become associated with music and the recruitment of musicians:

> . . . participation in music may be a voluntary activity or an obligation imposed by one's membership in a social group. Such social groups may be descent groups (a group of people who trace their ancestry back to the same person), or it may be any group based on the broader societal classifications of age, sex, interest, or occupation (1974, 35).[12]

Group association in Africa may be responsible for the image held here of African male drummers. Staged performances tend to perpetuate the thinking that drumming is a male dominated concept. Performing African groups regularly present staged renderings of male

societies such as hunters and warriors. The festive atmosphere represented when hunters and warriers return home is a powerful image in
African life for African-Americans. Group affiliations may be highly
regulated, but certain festivals may not. Social events such as these
draw on professional and non-professional musicians from the community. One might easily see both male and female singers and dancers,
but generally male drummers. African writer and musician Francis
Bebey spoke of secret male societies, the Poro, among the Senufo in
Ivory Coast, Burkina Faso, and Mali, and their use of drums and masks:

> Masks and certain musical instruments are also kept in the sacred
> wood and are only brought out when they are needed for a partic-
> ular rite. These musical instruments, especially the drums, are
> normally played by men only, as is the case in most African societies.[13]

Nketia describes a similar occurrence:

> The membership of a particular royal ensemble or responsibility for
> particular music may be organized on the basis of kinship or ter-
> ritory. A given household may be made responsible for maintaining
> a particular musical tradition . . . In Dagomba country, for instance,
> the son of every player of the hourglass drum is expected to become
> a drummer. The daughter of a drummer is released from this obliga-
> tion, but she must send a son to replace her when she has one.[14]

Bebey included several drums associated with female drummers.
One of the instruments played by women is the water drum or "Gi
dunu" found among the Senufo as well as the Malinke of Guinea, Mali,
and Sénégal. This "consists of two large hemispheric calabashes
(gourds) that are cut in half and filled with water. They are placed side
by side, and two smaller upturned half calabashes float on the water"
(Bebey 1975, 101-102).[15] This instrument is played with a stick or with
the hands striking the upturned gourd. The calabash is a common item
used by women in cooking or for carrying a variety of things. The fact
that it can always be found in their daily activities makes this a logical
instrument for music making. Bebey also pictures a woman playing a
friction-drum from Congo and women from Niger drumming and clap-
ping their hands to provide rhythmic accompaniment to a song.

Sénégalese master sabar drummer Doudou N'Diaye Rose formed a
sabar ensemble using his thirty-one children and three wives, and by
doing so, broke with the generally accepted tradition in Sénégal in
which women did not play the sabar drums. According to Rose, he was

the first to establish a drumming class for boys and girls. We have seen that daughters born into drumming families readily take up drumming and perform well. Part of their community responsibility is to pass these skills onto their male children if they have no brothers.

During performances by the National Ballet of Guinea as part of an international tour in 1992, part of the production involved female dancers playing the tama (an hourglass shaped drum recognized in the United States as the "talking drum"). This drum is small, held under the arm, and struck with a curved stick. The probable intent was theatrical impact, but the image was there. No women in the production were seen playing the djimbe. There have been many suggestions regarding which drums women can or have played, but the djimbe has not been included among them.

The Dance and the Dancer

The Dance Class

The spaces used for dance classes are usually square or rectangular in shape. Participants normally dance in lines of three or more across, having enough rows to accommodate all in attendance. The instructor typically demonstrates the movement to be executed. He or she is then followed by the class either in block formation or by rows. Dance classes are not generally considered spectator events in the United States. When people are permitted to observe, there are usually firm restrictions regarding behavior in the class area. There is usually social interaction between dancers, or dancers and friends, who might have come as observers while the dance participants prepare for class. The instructor may be male or female but generally there are more female students than males in the class. On many occasions, there were no male dancers participating at all.

The following observations were made during dance classes held in Atlanta, New York, Philadelphia, Washington D.C., Los Angeles, Phoenix, and Tucson. These sessions involved African-Americans as well as students from a variety of ethnic backgrounds.

Preparation for Dance

In the United States, there is a recommended ritual known as the "warm up," a period which includes stretching movements and cardiovascular/aerobic activities. Recorded music, drumming, or simple verbal instructions are options for this segment. In most settings, physical preparation before dancing is recommended or at least encouraged by the teacher or leader in order to avoid possible injury. Two approaches to warming up exist in dance classes and pre-performance sessions. Each approach to warming-up seems dependent on the dance leader or teacher's background. The first approach was used by Africans teaching dance classes in the United States. African teachers generally use actual dance movements or modified dance movements for the warm-up exercise. Malang Bayo of Sénégal led his warm-up sessions to recorded music (Sénégalese popular music) and used Mande movements as part of the session. In workshops conducted by visiting African artists/instructors, the warm-up ritual was often left to the local dance leader or instructor. In a dance class for visiting Americans taken in Sénégal with Sénégalese dancer Diop, students asked for warm-up exercises before the actual dance instruction began. Although Diop led the warm up period, she was clearly not at ease with the practice. In observing African dancers in Africa and the United States, warming up is rarely part of their routine.

The second approach to warming up, followed by many African-Americans as instructors, tends to use preparatory exercises that one might observe in the athletic arena, for example, exercises for stretching muscles and movements to extend flexibility. A few of these exercises may apply generally to the dance, possibly for coordination or multi-patterned movement sequences using different parts of the body. In many instances, they were not dance specific in nature. An important note was that none of the warm-up activities observed resembled those employed by western classically trained dancers, which I believe reflects the basic nature of the dance.

There are African-Americans, Primus, Dunham, and others, who have taken the concept of warming up in western dance culture and have developed warm-up exercises specifically for African dance. An example can be found in techniques developed by dancer/historian Kariamu Welsh Asante. The Mfundalai technique which she has been developing since 1975 includes movement characteristics consistent with general African dance techniques. This approach also holds concern for the dancer's health and well-being as a central concept.[16] African-American dancer, Diarra (1990), suggested that warm-up exercises are particularly important for Americans because the average American's lifestyle does not promote the strengths, flexibility, and postures found or needed in African dance. He expressed a genuine concern for protection against hyperextension and damage to the elbow, shoulder, and knee.

Posture

The basic posture used by both Africans and African-Americans reveals preferences related to their cultural norms. These preferences are tied to their respective cultural aesthetic. To review briefly, many of the Mande dances are performed with the basic body alignment of knees bent, a forward pelvic and waist tilt, shoulder section erect, and head up. In the United States, the physical demands in lifestyle and environmental conditions leading to this posture are no longer relevant to a majority of African-Americans. Also, there are few other visual examples of this posture in contemporary culture. In dance warm-up sessions, this basic posture is sometimes reinforced for non-African dancers. Observations made in dance classes and performances showed that the general posture used by African-Americans is more erect than Africans observed in intense performance situations. The knees are always bent to a degree as described in the earlier section on dance; however, with African-American dance students, the degree of flex is slight.

Each dance teacher was asked about this basic posture as used by African-American dancers. A general description included moderate flex in the knees, and a moderate pelvic tilt with a preference for an

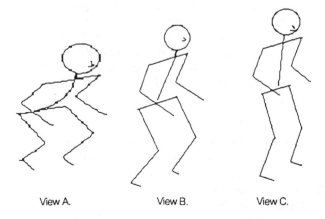

View A.   View B.   View C.

Figure 3.6
African and African-American Postures in Mandiani.

upright torso. One could argue that the degree of expertise present or lacking in the dance student is responsible for the differences in posture; however, this is an easily obtainable characteristic if presented and reinforced in class by the teachers. The contention is that this posture is not the highest priority for many teachers or students. *Figure 3.6* offers three examples of posture for the dance Mandiani. View "A" is an observation made of African dancers in an intense performance environment while views "B" and "C" are typical of dancers seen in Africa in situations other than a performance application and generally in the United States in class and performance.

View A represents the intense African dancer in the performance setting, such as a concert event for the professional dancer, or actual community celebrations.[17] In these contexts, there is often a competitive spirit while dancing Mandiani and dancers regularly attempt to go one step further than the previous dancer. At that instant there is an electrifying sensation generated between the drummer and dancer which is felt throughout the audience.

There are African-American dancers who are likely to assume this intense posture. These dancers do not however represent the majority of African-American dancers I have seen in the class or concert venue. Even those dancers who have been involved in Mande dance for many years may not use the extreme posture illustrated in View A. Specific questions were asked to discern which of these postures was preferred by American students and teachers. The teachers we talked to, Africans and African-Americans, accepted the entire range of postures illustrated. Many students and several performers expressed either discomfort or physical difficulty in executing the dance step using the posture in View A. For these individuals, there was a preference for the more erect stance.

Movement

"The movements in African dances are sensuous, sexy, and free." These are a few of the words used by observers of, and participants in, African dance as I interviewed American audiences and participants for this study. In contrast, the most frequent comments made by African-Americans about the dance Mandiani were that these movements are strong, vigorous, and physically demanding. Perceptions of movement and meaning in a movement are often culture specific. A final performance does not always reflect the aesthetic position of the entire group. Artistic and musical directors, along with choreographers, make the decisions which are put forth in the final production. The performer is then restricted to the parameters set by the directors. Even when contextual explanations are available, viewers may still be biased by their own perceptions which often do not include the total cultural significance of a movement.

The administrative personnel who establish the basic ensemble approach usually come from the ranks of the musicians and dancers who perform African music and dance in the United States. From my conversations with these individuals, there is a preference for movements that fall into one or more of the following categories: quick and athletic movements (with jumps and spins), movements that show the body, movements that extend the body, movements that are grounded and low, and movements with a sensual quality.

Movements that are Quick and Athletic

The notion that African dance is exercise is prominent among students and observers alike. There are a number of dance/exercise courses which routinely teach movements requiring the same athletic abilities as many of the Mande dances. In recent years, Afro-aerobic classes have been developed. No doubt these classes are targeted toward a clientele from or sympathetic to Afrocentric thought. These classes are in some ways reminiscent of the interpretive dance classes of the 1950s and 1960s. The people in attendance are not usually the same individuals who take African dance classes or who are members of a performing African dance ensemble.

Most of the students in an African dance class are at least in part interested in the cultural association with Africa. There may be many other personal reasons for their involvement such as social relationships, a version of self-administered emotional therapy, and for many the physical exercise as well. These individuals, usually women, vary from young adults to middle age. The male preference is to associate with drumming. Although drummers will occasionally feign dance, it is rarely a full-hearted attempt. Consequently, the larger representation in the typical African dance class is female. Out of this group, most participants hold the aspect of physical conditioning as one of the primary benefits of their commitment. Rarely are the benefits of grace, poise, posture, coordination, or other results associated with western dance classes used as justification for taking classes in African dance. The individuals involved with African dance describe themselves as physical people. Several dancers admitted that if they were not involved in

African dance, they would be involved in some other type of physical activity.

The prevailing attitude is supportive what the Mande dance style can do for the body, and what is required of the body in performing the movements. Power and strength are key elements considered by men and women dancers. For the women it is an opportunity to develop and display strength that may not be comfortably displayed in other cultural settings. Many males interested in dancing Mandiani and other Mande dances do not believe these dances compromise their masculinity even though ethnic or staged dance is not an activity usually undertaken by African-American males. The similarity in the physical demands of Mandiani and popular dance is a key issue for young men. The masculine image is upheld by the physical nature of both dance styles.

Movements that Show the Body

Generally, when dancers speak of articulation, they are referring to a stylized movement or how particular parts of the body are used to produce a specific shape or "picture." For dancers, very specific extremity joints such as the wrist or knee are articulated to produce specific shapes. General discussions about movement will invariably require the individuals to illustrate the dance by progressing through a series of static positions with a particular moment representing the absolute pose. This approach to illustrating dance movement is typically western. The reference to pose amplifies the importance of personal image. Portia Maultsby cited the importance of dress as part of the African-American performance aesthetic in "Africanisms in African-American Music" and this should also include the importance placed on being seen by other ensemble members and non-performers. The concept of "pose" as it is employed in the dance class, rehearsal, and performance supports this idea. The concept of follow-through, or continuous movement, is still required or dancers to to reverse themselves or terminate and proceed to the next movement. Momentary stops will still occur within the dance "phrase."

Abrupt or quick motions might be referred to as hard or angular. In this instance, the extremities are extended and move sharply from position to position. For those dancers who are attracted to the quickness of Mandiani, the concept of pose in the execution of the dance is the highest order in aesthetic preference. Many of the movements used in this dance require a quick reversal of direction which creates a momentary pose. Among African-Americans, a soft interpretation of the Mandiani movement presented in *Figures 2.4* through *2.7* would indicate that the dancer is not executing the movement in the aggressive character of the dance. For a "soft" movement, the extremity should not be rigidly articulated, rather it is moved or held in a relaxed manner. "Soft" might also express flowing from position to position without an abrupt fixation throughout the full range of the gesture. Soft movements are not typically selected by dancers for Mandiani.

The idea of hurling one's body or extremities through space or extending them physically beyond one's accepted personal space is recognized in western cultures as a dramatic feature of Mande dance. This single attribute has been associated with Sénégalese dance for many years in the United States. In watching this free and unrestricted dance style, one could easily get the impression that the dance or the dancer has no specific choreographic direction for the hands or arms. From the Mande perspective, these gestures simply happen as a result of the movements in the dance. Among dancers with European training, a conscious effort is made to identify specific movements and gestures for the head, arms, hands, and other body parts. Dance teachers from the Mande cultures often give little more than basic directions for these movements.[18] This freedom of movement is captured by relatively few African-American students in the dance class. Often the directions given are used to designate where the gestures begin and end, however there is little guidance given to increase idiomatic movements.

Dance teachers are concerned with dance related injury and often times this concern is offered as justification for limiting or controlling motion. Diarra was one of the teachers who pointed out that one's impression of what is being done within the dance gesture may not include the controls needed, and these controls are necessary for safety. Diarra's system of "Afrokinesthetics" was created for this purpose. He firmly insists that control of the body allows the dancer to articulate the movement safely. To project an image of unbridled execution of dance movements becomes a very meticulous study. There are African-American dancers who are able to project the impression of spontaneity and still exercise their concerns for control.

Movements that are Grounded and Low

"Grounded" and "low" are terms used by dance scholars and researchers to describe some African and African-American dance styles. Grounded is used to indicate that the dancer's feet remain in contact with the ground. When describing movements this way the analyst usually refers to a shuffling or dragging movement with the feet. "Low" often refers to the position of the upper body which is contracted along with bent knees. The dance Mandiani, as it was originally viewed in the United States, did not easily fit the grounded and low description.

The prominent movement characteristic of this dance is buoyancy. This, in addition to holding the arms extended and quick movements, often gives the impression of flight rather than groundedness. Of course, all viewpoints are subject to a variety of interpretations. Kariamu Welsh Asante had this opinion when asked about the seeming contradiction between Mandiani and the general descriptions of African dance. Asante echoed the words Pearl Primus used in a lecture given at the Black Arts Festival held in Atlanta in 1990 when she said, "African dance always relates to the earth. . . . If you leave it, you must return." During Primus' lecture on dance, a person in the audience observed that in most of the photographs taken of Primus, she was in the air with jumps and leaps. Primus responded by saying even though you may leave the ground, "you must always return to the earth."

In either case, dance movement within the African-American community has always gravitated toward highly animated gestures and expressions. The generation that first seized the dance Mandiani was undoubtedly attracted to the dance because of the visually intense activity and a style which was not a part of the African-American community. The dances of the swing era may have suggested these animated qualities, and certainly, contemporary popular dances exhibit many of these same animated qualities.

Movements with a Sensual Quality

Sensual qualities typically are not displayed in the movements which are chosen to illustrate the continuity between the African and African-American interpretations of the dance Mandiani. However, this is not to say there are no movements which could fall into this category. Movements which are usually labeled sensual or sexy are movements that, in part, require a pelvic thrust, a shimmy, or an undulating spine. It is interesting that many of the choreographed portions of the dance Mandiani in the United States and Africa do not feature sensual movement styles. They do exist. Sensuality in a dance movement may have implications which reach far beyond immediate or personal settings. Displays of sensuality generally do not carry negative connotations in indigenous cultures. Often, a solo dancer will choose a movement from one of these styles. The choice of these "sensual" movements in the African culture generally addresses the idea of fertility, virility, and the dancer's preparedness for marriage. In the United States, these steps are often selected by younger dancers. Senior dancers with gregarious personalities also tend to select from this movement's category.

Technique

The technique required for dance activity is as much a mental process as it is a physical one. The dancer must know intellectually how the movements fit into the rhythmic structure, and must also have the physical control to articulate these movements in the proper manner. There are several levels of control and many points in a movement which must be used to determine proper execution. The grand gestures in Mandiani conform to the primary rhythm patterns played by the drums. On this level, the overall flow of music and motion is perceived in much the same way by both musicians and dancers. There are rhythmic subdivisions which present a multi-layered series of timing points. With this rhythmic stratification, most, if not all, of the points of articulation in the dance movement can be directly related to drumming patterns. Dancers who have studied modern dance, or those with formal European dance training, are quick to point out that the approaches used in African dance are not the same as those used in modern dance. In modern dance, the movement gestures are not always conceived to be precisely articulated with musical events and rhythms. It most often happens that in modern dance, musical events may not be closely related to dance at all.

Gesture articulation in African dance can be analyzed rhythmically along with other components found in the music structure and can be viewed as part of the polyrhythmic structure found in the music. The considerations of direction, timing, weight placement, body positioning, movement in general, projection, thrust, and velocity can be considered part of the rhythmic structure in the same way that the drummer's hands and sticks striking the drum can be considered to ensure the correct rhythmic articulation. In essence, dancers and drummers have the same obligation in presenting their particular visual or sonic rhythms. The dancer must consider when to initiate and complete movements in order for the drum rhythm and the dance movements to occur in the right place.

There are points in posture, movements, and the rhythmic interpretation of movements in African dance which can be used to differentiate between African-American and African dancers. A few of these distinguishing characteristics were discussed with dance teachers Sherriff, Asante, Bayo, and Konte during interviews in California, Arizona, and New York. These characteristics include:

① *The triplet foot pattern*

② *The forward pelvic tilt*

③ *The African-American bounce*

④ *Stylized Sénégalese arm and wrist movements*

⑤ *Subtle gestures by African dancers*

⑥ *Sénégalese foot placement and position*

① The triplet (see Chapter Two, *Figure 2.4*) is one of the fundamental components in the dance Mandiani. These patterns are based on the lowest rhythmic strata or set of timing points in the duplet subdivision of the dance.[19] Observation is the principal method used for assimilating or learning movement. To date, there is no universal language for African dance instruction. With imitation as the primary procedure for acquiring these skills, the differences in perception between Africans and African-Americans are distinguishable in the amount of new data that must be internalized with or without the benefit of similar kinetic nuances found in the indigenous dance culture.

Quite often, dance teachers will decide, after a period of time, to accept an inaccurate level of performance rather than belabor the point. In several classes dedicated to the dance Mandiani, the triplet foot pattern was performed by Assane Konte but was not separated from his explanation of the total dance gesture. His instructions to the class were to stay on the balls of their feet, weight forward, and keep light. Konte's analysis of the movement included the grand gestures. He believed that the continuing motion, rapid tempo, and rhythmic response required to alternate the pattern from the right foot to the left would subsequently achieve this objective. When students totally comprehended Konte's instructions, the subtleties of the movement were questioned. His response was, "The finer points will come from doing the dance." While performing this gesture, all Sénégalese dancers observed executed the rapid rhythmic subdivision. However, this was not true of all African-American dancers.

② "The forward incline of the upper body (forward pelvic tilt) is another common characteristic of African dance." This tilt is very natural among many Africans who assume this posture for dance because it is a common work posture used in agricultural societies. In contrast this forward incline is quite unnatural for contemporary African-Americans. All of the dance teachers commented that it was another one of the characteristics of African dance that requires special attention when teaching. As complex as many contemporary dances have become, they are generally executed with the torso upright.

③ "There is this African-American bounce (an up and down motion initiated in the knees) that often appears in this country that we have to eliminate." When teaching the dance Fanga, Asante addressed this movement as inappropriate for African dance.[20] This bounce appears frequently in the movements associated with choirs in the African-American church. A similar movement is used by background singers for many popular African-American artists or commercial pop artists influenced by African-American culture.

④ "There is a stylized Sénégalese arm movement and wrist articulation." Comments in reference to how the wrist and arm should be used were made in a workshop conducted by Nafisa Sharriff, as well as classes given by Konte and Bayo. Their comments were made in an effort to get their students to project the cavalier or flamboyant quality in Mande dance. Often the directions to articulate a turn of the wrist or a flip of the head or hand to end a movement are intended to create a sense of style or flair with the dance. Bayo, as part of his warm-up routine, includes a great deal of work on the musculature needed to produce subtle movements in the wrists, hands, and fingers. He has clearly found the need for this particular ability important and has dedicated time in the class to develop this ability in his students.[21] These gestures can be seen in outstanding African-American dancers but rarely in the average performer or dance student. The ability to regularly produce more subtle articulations is present in the dancers with many years of experience in the Mande style and those who have dedicated a major portion of their dance experience to these movements. In many instances, these subtle gestures can be traced to their primary dance mentor.

⑤ A few general observations can be made about the subtle gestures seen in Africans as they dance Mandiani and their inclusion or exclusion by African-American dancers. In Africa, individual dancers often have their own movement idiosyncrasies. These characteristics can often take on a communal dimension in that many of the community members may adopt a particular characteristic that is not present in other dance communities. One such characteristic was present among members of a dance group seen in the summer of 1992 in Kaolack, Sénégal, directed by Omar Thiam. Several dancers, male and female, tilted their heads upward with their eyes rolled back. One of the idiosyncrasies of dancer Assane Konte is a quick shake of the head at the beginning of each movement when dancing with high intensity. It is interesting to note that particular characteristic was adopted by many of Konte's students.

Idiosyncratic gestures certainly add personality to a dance movement, however, there are more basic mechanical actions which are essential to the movement chosen for this study. Several of these mechanical characteristics are often missed by dance students. These characteristics include retaining buoyancy by carrying the weight on the balls of the foot. Another characteristic which is missed by many African-American dancers is a body contraction while also executing a jump. When well executed, the lower half of the body may attain heights of fifteen to twenty inches while the level of the head is unchanged. Missed perceptions of weight placement and direction can cause a dance movement to take on a labored rather than an effortless appearance.

I wanted to understand why these gestures were not captured by many African-Americans. Several explanations are possible: 1) the average dance student does not see the subtleties in the movements or cannot reproduce them. In this instance, it is possible that one must concentrate so intently on the grand gesture that it is not possible to see the subtleties in the movements. This may well be the primary explanation for limited sensitivities to fine motor gestures; 2) it is possible that many of the African-American dancers unable to reproduce these movements do not have the muscle control or flexibility required to do so; and 3) the motivation that brings students to a particular dance class may not be solely to learn the dance, but may be an effort to address or to escape other physical, and/or psychological pressures.

Several examples can be used to illustrate points one and two. "Many African-American dancers don't understand the follow through of the neck and head as a continuation of the spine." This comment was made by two instructors, Melvin Deal and Abubakr Diarra. What is being referred to here is an undulating quality which begins as a wave motion in the lower back and follows through the spine and neck which does not end until this action causes the head to react. Both dancers addressed the limited movement characteristics of African-Americans, and both offered slightly different solutions. Deal was quite adamant when he said, "Learning the dance begins with the eyes. You have to see me before you can repeat the dance movement." Diarra was very concerned with health issues. With a detailed explanation of how the muscles function and are connected, Diarra contends that only those dancers prepared for the explanation would be ready to attempt the movement:

> Diarra—The movement, it's a problem of mechanics. I have developed a technique I call Afro-Kinesthetic and possibly put both African and western movement styles together in preparing my class. It is very necessary because there are a lot of things that are happening to the body that the eye does not see. You may see me move, but you have to feel for yourself and see for yourself what exactly it is that I am doing. People years ago, when I started, could not or did not do what I do now. Those things I took upon myself to learn, I did not because somebody said you're supposed to do it this way, but because many of the things I was being shown didn't feel right to me. You can't really mix ballet, modern, and tap with African dance because you're using different lines. You're using different muscles and the body has to be toned differently.

> Sunkett—You see that there is a real physical difference between western and African dance?

> Diarra—Mixing these dance styles is a real problem because when these western movements become merged with African movements, it takes the purity from the African style. You see, when I'm dancing, it's my soul that I share, or a part of it. You can't see it if I'm just sitting here, so that when I'm dancing you do, you feel it, that's very necessary in African movement; it's very necessary. A lot of movements have been adopted to this plane, this wood and Euro concrete, so you have to retrain the body. I have friends from Africa whose feet are permanently damaged now because they were never trained to use this kind of surface.

⑥ "Sénégalese foot placement and position is not just what you see." In a workshop conducted by Assane Konte, students in the class noticed the height achieved in his leaps and the effortless quality in his dancing. Konte was quick to describe the differences between the manner in which he and the students supported their weight with their feet and the flex of the knees while dancing. The American students tended to place their feet flat on the floor and use minimal flex if any in the knees. According to Konte, "You cannot get light (lift) from this position." The spring comes from the knees, the arches, and then the balls of the feet. "It may look like my foot is flat, but it's not." Each of these stylistic articulations represent difficult aspects of Mande dance for American students. These detailed understandings are foreign to many African-Americans because they are not part of their aesthetic vocabulary. Arguments have been advanced that females stand a better chance of reproducing these gestures because in western culture females are much more aware of their bodies from an early age. Their fine motor skills and general control over movement are developed more quickly than males as a result.

Staging

In the United States Mandiani is performed out of its original cultural context. Several problems result when attempting to use a circle configuration in the western performance arena. First, if dancing in a circle on an American stage, it is difficult for all of the performers to be seen. Second, if the soloist were to move to the center of the circle to dance, the audience would lose sight of that individual. Finally, the dancers would never fully face front if the circle were the only configuration used. Performances of Mandiani in the United States are directed toward the audience. Most performing companies use Mandiani as a focal point in their presentation. Quite often, the dance begins with a drum signal while the drummers are positioned at the rear or side of the stage. Immediately following the signal, the dancers move quickly to a pre-arranged position. Semi-circles, lines, or variants of the line formations are the norm. These formations allow the audiences to see each dancer. Both of these settings regulate the way the dance will be presented.

The concept of choreography as it is viewed by African national companies and African-Americans is stringent. Performing groups generally subscribe to the notion that everyone should dance the same movement in choreographed sections of the dance. An individual dancing a solo may choose or be assigned a particular step to perform but they are not encouraged to invent movements. The dance steps are performed in chorus, therefore, choreographers concern themselves with how easily one movement flows to another. A drastic approach to the notion of conformity was suggested by one choreographer when he said, "If you have someone who does the dance much better than everyone else, you should put that person in the back so that the audience's attention would not be drawn to that person."

Because Mandiani requires sustained energy levels for most steps, choreographers also concern themselves with "rest steps" which give the dancers a chance to catch their breath and prepare for the next flurry of movements. This is not a concern in the village because dancers enter the dance arena for their solo and exit at will. The solo may not last very long and there is plenty of time to rest at the perimeter of the circle.

Mental State

Dance teachers are in touch with a greater number of community members than drum instructors or other musicians. As dance teachers, they may also find themselves in the position of counselor to many of their students. It has been noted that many students may have issues affecting their personal life when they come to class. These individuals often look to music and dance activity as an avenue of escape from the routine of daily lifestyle, or as a possible way to gain access to the healing properties believed to be carried in African art forms. In order to have an effective class, dance instructors must often take an active part in the process leading toward the resolution or settling of conflicts. All dance teachers have great concerns about the mental state of their students.

Sharriff encounters students who enter a dance class with motivations beyond learning the dance being taught. In our discussion over how the teacher might handle various problems a student might bring to class, she said, "My philosophy in class is 'you've gotta' have fun.' If students comes into my class with personal problems, the class may be therapeutic for them. They can leave with a feeling of accomplishment."

Deal has his own understanding of student problems. "Social pressures have created a sense of confusion and frustration in many people which has led them to get involved with African dance as a healing tool. I have to reorient many students in order for them to learn effectively." According to Deal, a significant number of African-Americans involved in African dance can be characterized as "Jump Junkies":

> These people enter a dance class looking for wild throwing and flinging of arms, across the floor progressions with wild movement, and they are not specifically concerned with technique and execution. There are many dance students who enter the class with personal problems and use this forum to escape momentarily.

Female dancers typically are much more open about personal issues, especially in what could easily be considered a closed circle of association. Within the class or ensemble, women will often share their opinions openly on personal or dance related themes. Male participants usually are much less open. During a discussion concerning Sénégambian cultural dances and the students in his classes, Deal continued:

> I specifically explain to my students that they are an image of
> the society in which they dwell. When people come in here
> disoriented, when they come overly anxious, when they come in
> here overly shy, they're products of the outside world and the
> reason they cannot get the dance movements is because they
> only hear what they want to hear as opposed to what I'm telling
> them. Many people who take African dance come in with a
> serious case of the 'fritties' so that when the drums start, they
> just want to jump around.

The African-American Community

Social Environment

The social arena for African-Americans interested in African dance traditionally has been in community centers located in less affluent neighborhoods and African-American communities located within the inner-city area. Generally, participants live in a cross section of neighborhoods within the city or suburbs, but meet for African dance activity in what is typically identified as the center of African-American existence. African drum and dance activity is always communal. Among African-Americans, and along with the attitude of community exhibited in these group sessions, there is the same friendly competitiveness among musicians and dancers as experienced in African communities.

According to several teachers such as Assane Konte, Melvin Deal, Abdulai Aziz Ahmed, and C.K. Ganyo, more often single males and females get involved with African music and dance to find social partners. There are parents who insist on participation by their children in order to enhance their cultural awareness, education, and social responsibility. Often, the children's classes meet before the adult sessions. If parent and child are involved, it becomes an extended family experience. Throughout the day, one can readily find children playing in the vicinity, even though they may not directly be involved in the drum and dance activity.

Several factors are considered by drum and dance teachers in choosing a venue for classes and rehearsals. First, the community must be tolerant of the drums, the range of sounds associated with the activity, and the resultant high level of pedestrian traffic. These classes are often attended by adults and their children, and there is a certain degree of clamor associated with the gatherings. The second consideration is to provide a venue centrally located and conveniently accessible for the participants. For many participants from the Black community, transportation is a primary concern in large urban settings since public conveyances are often the principal mode of transportation available for these individuals.

The participants involved in this cultural and social activity also believe that it should take place in a culturally relevant environment. Whether the surrounding community is actively participating or not, there is a concern for relevance to the community. This concern may explain why there is a low level of participation among African-American students on college and university campuses. The environment associated with academic institutions, the general ethnic make-up of the student population, and resultant social climate are not the preferred settings for college aged African-Americans to engage in these socio-cultural activities. When these classes take place within the preferred environment, individuals outside of the African-American community exhibit reluctance to venture into these communities where African music and dance are commonly presented. Sensitivity to ethnic association and social attitudes prevent many non-African-Americans from attending classes located in ethnically specific neighborhoods.

In the African-American community, the pursuit of African culture or African related culture is usually recreational and not vocational. There are very few artists who can declare the income generated solely from this art form constitutes a large enough income to sustain an acceptable lifestyle. Participants were asked why they chose the Mande style dances. The participants considered their involvement in dances such as Mandiani a physical commitment worthy of their efforts. Each individual took great satisfaction and gratification in Mandiani because of the high physical and technical demands made on dancers and drummers. Also, participants were happy with the opportunities for peer interaction and comradeship. For drummers, playing parts that reflected equal value in musical importance was significant. For dancers, social and recreational dances such as Mandiani tend to offer the

most freedom of expression. This feeling was shared by the drummers
as well. If there are little or no choreographic or programming constraints placed on the activity, drumming and dancing provides a
vehicle for personal expression in spite of the restrictions of the dance
movements and drum parts.

For drummers, the interpretation of parts offers a sense of independence or autonomy even though each part is specific. Although each
part should be played correctly, one part is not dependent upon
another; therefore, each part is important. Once the music has begun
and the basic dance movement established, the individuals involved express pleasure in the sense of freedom afforded them while interpreting
their drum parts or dance movements. An established practice at the
end of the dance class offers each participant the chance to dance a solo.
Each student is free to create their movements from the material
presented in that day's class, or create movements of their own. Among
female dancers, there is usually open acknowledgment of those who
skillfully execute solo steps. With male dancers, the competitive spirit is
often very obvious. It seems to be important with male dancers to maintain an image of control and effortlessness while dancing in spite of the
energy required to perform. This attitude of control is also seen in the
reserved and often silent acknowledgment for the prowess of other
male dancers in the session.

Hierarchy and Personalities

In any group of people, leaders and followers will emerge, some by
choice and others by community acknowledgment. Gender issues have
already been mentioned ín reference to the choice between instru-
mentalist or dancer. Is there a cultural aesthetic at work in developing
the administrative hierarchy? Consider the areas of administrative acceptance and political importance within the ensemble or class. They
are most often tied to individual personalities dedicated to the art and
less governed by leadership ability. This is not to say that an individual
can emerge a leader without those qualities normally associated with
leadership, but, the ability to relate on an interpersonal level can distinguish a leader of people in these groups from a person in control of
business interests.

Public performance and working with people cannot be devoid of
personality issues, particularly when it is difficult to guarantee an artist
stability of employment or substantial revenues for performing. Control
over inappropriate conduct or drastically abnormal behavior is ad-

ministered by the leadership with support by group acknowledgment. Politics are rarely dictatorial. There are usually rules of conduct in place. The communal whole is often a mitigating body. Procedures are established for the course of events in classes or performance events, however, there is a reasonable tolerance to deviation. Flexibility and the acceptance of slight irregularities are apparent. Conversations noted between dancers showed an interest in each other's well being and their willingness to discuss problems openly. Regardless of the number of dancers present at the community dance classes, there was a general sense of community.

There are different criteria used for distinguishing leaders in classes and in performing ensembles. The criteria are developed among the students attending classes or the ensemble members, and they are not necessarily solidified in either setting before the class or ensemble is established and operating for a period of time. Leadership generally resides in those individuals having the greatest experience in the art form. Talented individuals will figure prominently in the instructional areas, but the appeal of a dance class and a performing ensemble is credited to the personalities of the teachers and administrative personnel. Many participants may be more willing to accept physical challenges and organizational shortcomings from a group which reflects strong human sensitivity rather than place themselves in situations that are highly structured but less personal. In the African-American community, a homogeneous group personality is a highly attractive commodity. In areas where there are two or more ensembles involved with African dance, the individuals possessing artistic commitment, interpersonal skills, and management abilities are usually those who attract the greater number of people. The success of African dance classes or performing groups is viewed by the community in terms of the human image in leadership, and the art product. Failure is almost always equated to poor management.

There are very few individuals who can afford to dedicate 100 per cent of their time and efforts to the teaching or performance of African music and dance. The leaders of classes or ensembles who have been successful make it very clear that they had to begin with little money. They offered services, either classes or performances, at no cost initially. Because of their commitment to art, some artists accept a lifestyle which would not be acceptable to others. For instance, these individuals may provide for themselves through artistic activity in a variety of areas.

Clearly, most of the participants in African music and dance view their involvement as a form of personal enrichment. Therefore, learning, teaching, and performing African music and dance is an elective activity rather than a mandated one. The participant's involvement reflects an aesthetic commitment of one's time and energies to the art form.

Members of the African-American community who become involved with a performance ensemble are concerned that their presentations are ethnically specific. The desire, in formal presentations of African music and dance, is that only persons with a demonstrable link to Africa or perceptible African lineage will represent the total body of performers. This claim to an ancestral right is not a prejudicial one. It is rather an act of communal solidarity and cultural awareness. Parents encourage their children to observe African cultural activities even though they may not want to participate in them. This is in part due to the lack of exposure to this art form in mainstream American society. In many parts of the United States, learning African music and dance is not limited by African-Americans to those within their ethnic group. Classes are often attended by a variety of individuals with varied ethnic backgrounds. However, African-Americans are not alone in the belief that the presentation of this art form is best represented by teachers, and performers with an appropriate visual image. City, state, and national arts organizations also support the presentation of ethnic arts by members of specific ethnic groups.

Human Interaction

Basic male and female roles are defined through their choices as drummers and dancers. Beyond that, women are involved because of the physical demands represented in the style, cultural association, cultural awareness, education, and/or physical exercise. Women who are attracted to the drum are usually attracted to the sound. It is rare that females pursue their curiosity for the instrument as performers. Many times those females who do explore this interest decide against playing the djimbe because of the growth of calluses that can be expected. Usually, those women interested in drumming select the diun diun which is played with a stick rather than the bare hands.

As seen in a number of male dancers, many males elect not to dance in performing ensembles. For them, dance is not generally viewed as a masculine activity in the United States. For many, staged dance performance is still equated to European ballet. In recent years, vernacular dance or street dancing has moved from the house party and night club to the concert stage with popular music artists often employing large groups of dancers, male and female. This current trend may be shifting the opinion of many potential male dancers. Those who choose to perform African dance are usually comfortable with the genre and often times reject the stereotype of the effeminate male dancer. The drum ensemble has typically been the arena for male participation. Hand drumming, still considered primitive by some, is an acceptable vehicle for artistic involvement in formal concert presentations. The competitive spirit within the ensemble is affirmation of the male drive for dominance in social situations.

In the majority of dance groups and classes in the United States the dancers meet in a space separate from the drummers for the first part of the session. There is typically time between the official beginning of class or rehearsal for preparatory activities such as warming up and the actual beginning of work. The social interaction between dancers is generally supportive, and there are usually veteran dancers available to assist in the orientation of newcomers to the classes. For most of the classes observed, this time for drummers is used for preliminary assignments and social interaction. This largely involves music issues, but there are occasional discussions related to non-musical topics. In the early development of djimbe ensembles in the United States, part of the preparation time was spent preparing and tuning the drums. This was accomplished by setting the drums in front of a portable heat source, typically a hot plate or small electric heater. These electrical devices are substitutes for the traditional drum fire. This was a treasured time for communing among the drummers, according to one drummer. The idea of not using heat to tune the drum has dissolved this "free" time to a large extent. Other devices such as heat guns have shortened the process even more so that the necessity to arrive or congregate early for many players has diminished greatly with less social time as a consequence.

With a performance as the focal event, time parameters are more closely adhered to and conversations are focused on performance concerns, costuming, potential problems or flaws in the performance, and possible solutions. Also, the concert environment tends to evoke a more determined or serious attitude for all concerned. The basic differences in attitude between the class and the performance setting depends upon the audience to whom the activity is directed. In a concert performance there is an understanding that it is at least fifty percent, if not totally, for the audience. The class is somewhat ambiguous because the persons to whom the activity is directed are: self, other participants, possibly observers, the instructor, or specific individuals targeted by the performer for personal or political reasons. These options may exist in various combinations with each performer.

A sense promoted in the African dance environment is that the dancers are performing in part for the drummers, and also the drummers can be inspired by and have a responsibility to the dance and/or the dancers. The interaction between drummers and dancers figures prominently in the lure of African music and dance to many participants, and it is important in the consideration of the community's aesthetic perception of the activity. For many performers, the audience is secondary to the drummer/dancer interaction. In a sense, the audience is invited into the domain of the performers. If drumming takes place immediately before an event, as it often does, it allows the drummers to solidify their ensemble sense. For the dancers, music provides the immediate atmosphere for the impending performance and sensitizes them to the accompanying ensemble. For the audience, this musical offering serves the same communicative purposes as its western counterparts, the overture or prelude which is meant to set the mood or create the atmosphere for the coming event.

Communication

A variety of interactive communication techniques and processes exist in African music and dance, and they are necessary for successful performances in class and on stage. These forms of communication manifest themselves through verbal and nonverbal means between drummers, dancers, and/or their respective leaders. Interactive communication reflects understandings based in historic and contemporary culture accepted as tradition, practice, expectation, spontaneity, creativity, and innovation.

Signals have evolved in each regional music language in Africa. Tradition provides the most basic framework for this kind of communication, and it is used similarly in both African and African-American cultures. There are language or signal based rhythms for communicating in the drum and dance ensemble. In this investigation of Mandiani, there is no evidence of a direct verbal translation for any of the drum rhythms. However, the processes and methods of communication, the cues and signals used between drummers or between drummers and dancers, are part of the basic format. It is in the musical cues, signals, and possibly the array of steps used that regional identities emerge.

Drummer Communication

Our objective here is to identify the various means by which communication takes place. In both the African and African-American drumming communities, rhythmic instruction is achieved through the use of vocal sounds or "nonsense syllables" known as vocables. To do so, each possible sound from the drum is given one corresponding vocal utterance.[22] Systems vary from culture to culture and in a few instances, the vocables used also indicate right or left hand. Babatunde Olatunji has presented workshops throughout the United States, and has introduced many drummers to the language he uses to transmit rhythms. Olatunji's vocable system is very simple and has only three basic sounds:

> tone —go; for a series of tone sounds use go and do
> bass — gun; for a series of bass sounds use gun dun
> slap — pac; for a series of slap sounds use pac ka

Dancer Communication

In village settings, verbal communication is minimal unless the dance is very stylized or ritualistic. There are concert circumstances in Africa and the United States in which the lead dancer verbally signals changes in movement. In this event, the dancers rely on an established vocal sound. Rarely is this an actual command, but a sound alerting dancers to upcoming position shifts or calling their attention to problems in staging. Basic procedures are established during practice sessions and these vocal sounds are usually adequate to direct corrections to any problems or effect any necessary changes. The lead drummer may or may not be required to respond to the dancer's signal. Other non-drummer initiated changes in dance sequence occur through prearranged choreographic settings. With this procedure, both the lead drummer and the lead dancer may present signals. These signals may serve to alert members of the ensemble, yet the movement precision is not dependent on these cues. There is interactive communication between drummers and dancers which is at the heart of the African drum and dance experience.

Collective Ensemble Communication

The lead drummer must establish an intuitive link with the lead dancer or dancers. Drummers must be aware of the physical demands inherent in dance steps and they must be sensitive to dancers. In less structured situations, the dance circle in the African village or the final portion of the dance class in the United States, the lead drummer must be able to sense the enthusiasm for a particular step and the level of fatigue exhibited by dancers. It is the drummer's responsibility to sense the appropriate time to change. It is part of the African tradition and the expectation in the United States that the lead drummer responds in this manner.

The break, as it is used in the signalling mode, can halt the motion completely and/or change the tempo. Both actions have their roots in traditional culture. Through the course of ceremonial or ritualistic events, for example, the dance may not be predetermined. It is probable that there are segments clearly identified through music and dance. If so, a signal is played by the lead drummer between each segment. In the performance of recreational music, the usual application for Mandiani, the challenge offered by the drummers to the dancers is to "catch the break" which clearly illustrates the play element in drumming and dance.

Both the musician and dancer may taunt one another by trying to go beyond the technical abilities or comprehension of their partner. The term "break" can also apply to a short segment in the music and dance which serves to interrupt the flow of a particular dance movement or offer a contrasting section. These sections are generally initiated and terminated choreographically with punctuations by the lead drummer. Another possible music variation used follows a general progression from slow to fast. It is the expectation that Mandiani will either be performed at a fast tempo from the very beginning, or alternately, it may begin at the normal performance tempo and accelerate to a speed which would almost defy execution.

Two possible directives are implied with the break as it is used in the performance of Mandiani. First, the break can serve to call dancers to the solo position on stage or into the center of the dance arena. Although it is the exception rather than the rule that Mandiani is danced informally in the United States, the format generally followed in the choreographed or staged professional versions of the dance still suggests the environment of the informal village context. These breaks are helpful in mounting presentations that are viewed by audiences as well rehearsed and "professionally" executed in the contemporary African-American context.

The breaks played for dance solos are intended to represent those occasions when the impromptu soloist enters the village dance arena. However, the reality of concert or staged performances often dictates a more rehearsed format in performing groups. Even though dancers and drummers may not "rehearse" as such for dance occasions in the village setting, familiarity among the participants creates an awareness of, and sensitivity to each person's individual style. At the end of the dancer's solo display, typically there is a simultaneous signal, premonition or sensed clue from the lead drummer and solo dancer which leads to a terminating gesture by the dancer which is articulated by the drummer. This gesture is part of the normal performance practice in concert production.

These simultaneous reactions are meant to be viewed as intuitive. Dane Archer explains nonverbal communication as based in one's culture and has labeled it the "social intelligence quotient."[23] Similar acts of perception are carried out on a daily basis to some degree in every culture. This social intelligence, according to Archer, is not strongly related to verbal intelligence or literacy, two concepts heavily depended upon in western culture. In folkloric cultures, this intuition is relatively easy if the two individuals have performed together in the past and are familiar with each other's "style," or are extremely familiar with the procedure.

Each drummer has a vocabulary or repertoire of rhythms which is used and that must be perceived and understood by the dancer. With this vocabulary, the drummer will create the hints or "sensed clues" used before initiating his signals. It is incumbent upon the dancer to develop his or her intelligence in aural perception to understand the drummer's language.

Conversely, the drummer's intelligence, as defined in Archer's terminology of nonverbal communication, resides in his or her ability to interpret visual hints communicated from the dancers. The drummer must be able to distinguish the physical development of movement in the performance context and to initiate the break in anticipation of the dancer's movement leading to the closing gesture. This closing will be drawn from the individual dancer's collection of gestures and approaches to movement completion. The drummer's ability to perceive these movements in the performance context is in direct correlation to his status as a good drummer.

Costuming

Authenticity

One salient aspect of African culture is clothing. In the performance of African dance in the United State, many people miss the insight on the culture that is brought to a performance by looking at clothing worn and thinking of it as costume. If this change in terminology is accepted, the cultural significance of clothing and its functions in folk or ethnic arts adds another dimension to the experience. With culturally specific attire the dynamics of continuity, change, and adaptation can follow the evolution of the people and period under consideration. Clothing is necessarily of interest for the performing artist.

"We are all children of our own time and cannot fail to interpret the old themes through the eyes, ears, and senses of today."[24] The interpretation of old themes in clothing has already shifted to contemporary materials, unless those articles are of spiritual or ritual importance. Being distanced from the source of African culture, tremendous efforts are made by African-American performers to reintroduce African culture to their own community. In this reintroduction, issues of authenticity are continually raised in regard to clothing. Natural evolution in Africa has dissolved much of the information that is sought. Information presented to audiences regarding what is accurate or appropriate in African clothing is gathered wherever it can be found. The only recourse for many is to explore parallels in contemporary cultures.

African clothing can be viewed in historical or contemporary contexts, or with reinterpreted applications of traditional themes. Two distinctly different effects occur when a garment either covers movement or amplifies movement in the visual presentation. Here we will focus on costume elements that contribute sound and visual enhancement to the rhythms and movements of the dance Mandiani. In the book *Costumes for the Dance* author Betty Joiner refers to rhythm in design, referring to the effect of costuming or clothes creating visual movement through line, mass, color, and texture. Our concern is with movement or visual phenomena which relate directly to the rhythm presented in the movement. In Mandiani, dance movement and instrumental rhythms operate together.

The articulation of rhythm is generally thought to be the province of the drum sound. In African music, rhythms may be produced by singers, dancers, or other audience members and can be "reflected by hand-clapping, foot stamping, or the repetition of certain rhythmic onomatopoeias that are all artifices that imitate the drum beat." Clothing can make both visual and sonic contributions to the music and dance. As long as there is some presentation of rhythm, be it drum, idiophone, hand claps, vocal activity, or visual representation, the procedures can be considered part of the rhythm ensemble. This is the concept which encourages the audience, dancer, singer and drum ensemble to coalesce.

The drum may contribute to a visual representation of rhythm through the motion of the drummer, along with creating sounds above and beyond its basic sound function when there are adornments attached. The drum may be draped with fabric, elaborately carved, or otherwise adorned. As the instrument is carried, the movement of these additions contributes to the visualization of rhythm. Devices attached to the drums such as the kesingkesings[25] can supply sound when the drummer is simply walking with the drum. These attachments are intended to enhance the sound and punctuate the rhythms as the drum is played. There are African-American djimbe players who do not like either the look or the rattle of these devices. For them, this additional sound is bothersome and obscures the true sound of the drum. The idea of a pure tone is not consistent with the African sensibility, but it is a part of western culture.

Instrumentalists and dancers may contribute to the sonic material with their personal clothing such as ankle, wrist, and arm ornaments. Many females in a variety of African cultures wear multiple strands of beads or beaded aprons around their waist according to their age and marital status. In some traditional societies, unmarried girls will wear multiple strands of beads around the waist to signify their availability to marry. Married women wear one beaded strand. In contemporary times, it is clear that traditional costumes are changing. It has been noted that with a few contemporary African women, the distinction between married and unmarried is purposefully obscured.

In certain traditional African cultures, accessories worn by females may have served to limit mobility and restrict their ability to travel any great distance beyond the village boundaries. Practices have changed in most places. The restrictive aspects of these ornaments and accessories have in many instances disappeared all together. For instance, light weight substitute materials have come into being, removing the original intent for ankle bracelets. Many of these ornaments and accessories that were a part of traditional African society are being put aside for western attire, particularly in the area of daily wear. Photographs of contemporary urban African culture show the use of multiple ornamental rings around ankles, legs, and arms which are made from light weight metals such as copper or aluminum. If worn while dancing, the rings will contribute to the sonic rhythm, regardless of the materials used to make them.

Fabric may not always be worn as clothing. It could be part of the general ensemble, but it can also have other significant and utilitarian functions. Three possibilities exist for the use of fabric as a costuming entity. The first possibility takes into consideration the amount of fabric used to make a garment. For important occasions such as a wedding, multiple layers of clothing might be worn. A wedding ensemble seen in Dakar, Sénégal, included a grand boubou (caftan), multiple seurres (skirts), and a moussr (head wrap) of brocade. With this style of clothing only the hands, feet, and face are exposed. While dancing dressed in this ensemble, many subtle movements are obscured but the motion of the fabric becomes a visual representation of the rhythm.

Second, women often wear multiple fabrics tied about their waist during everyday activities. These fabrics can be used for carrying objects, or children. This multi-layering is usually related to the age group. Teenaged and young adult women generally wear one or two seurres. When they dance, one piece of fabric is rhythmically manipulated. Movements are not totally hidden and the flurry of fabric presents motion that can be rhythm based. The third possibility is a separate piece of cloth or the edge of the outer most seurre which is held and manipulated while dancing to visually extend the movement, thereby articulating the rhythm as well. In Kaolack, Sénégal, a young girl wearing a blouse and a single seurre, proclaimed by other residents of the compound to be the best dancer in the compound, would not dance without an additional piece of fabric wrapped around her waist which she manipulated rhythmically through each dance.

Michael Huet photographed a sparsely clad young girl performing movements of the "Zoua Dance" from the Guéré of Côte D'Ivoire.[26] His description referred to the dancer as "brandishing" a scarf. In this dance, the movement is slow at first and quickens as the dancer tries to impose her own rhythm on the drummer. The combination of movement and fabric in hand represents the visual control of tempo. Even though using a piece of fabric or manipulating the corner of the seurre might add a visual dynamic to the dance, these options are not regularly used by African-American dancers.

Two extremes in clothing style or body covering deserve consideration. The first is the act of totally covering the body, leaving little or no physical suggestion of the human form. In this event, the garment or covering, its movement, and its manipulation become the primary focus of attention and not the person inside. Many masked dances in Africa should be considered in this light. The garments or masks interpret the rhythm in the way they move and should be seen as part of the dance. There may be certain sounds that are made or generated from the covering. The second possibility uses the opposite approach making every movement of the body a contributor to visualized rhythm. In these instances, the dancer wears minimal clothing. The dancer does not want to obscure the various parts of the body or specific garments. Accessories and hand held objects might be used to amplify or extend the movement.

Alan Lomax talked about the polyrhythmic movement of the Dogon in his work on choreometrics attempting to define and categorize movement based on cultural phenomena.[27] Dance researchers speak about this categorization with rhythmic terms like pulse, staccato, strong and weak accents, etc. Similar comments are made about African-American culture. Fashion is also used when speaking of clothing in African-American popular dance styles. Clothes for dancing are often selected specifically to enhance the dance movements. However, the manipulation of garments or a separate piece of cloth does not appear to have the same importance in African dance performed by African-Americans as it does for the Mande cultures. African-American dancers will use only moderate amounts of fabric for clothing while performing African dance, usually wearing only one layer as opposed to multiple layers of clothing.

Materials Used

Fabric chosen to make African clothing is a concern that African-Americans regularly address. A major issue is how to get African print fabrics and designs. The resolution is multifaceted because what is perceived in the United States as desirable and even coveted for performance clothing is often beyond affordablity for performing groups in the countries where these dances originate. Also, many of those items used regularly by native African designers and costume builders in the past are no longer readily available in their countries. If a performing company of African-Americans wanted to stage an African-style ceremony in the United States, it is understood that the event would require the participants to wear their best and finest attire, as would their African counterparts. In reality, many of the performing groups in Africa would not use fabrics or materials of such quality for staged presentations either because of the fragile nature of the material, or the cost factors. African audiences can accept a lower quality in fabric because there is an understanding of what is expected and/or suggested in clothing in the culture and it is not necessary to reproduce all of the idiomatic appointments.

The effort to acquire printed fabrics and other high quality textiles, and the efforts to recreate events down to the smallest known details, is then a part of the American sensibility. Many performing groups aggressively attempt to acquire fabrics from African countries. The irony is that many fabrics used for the finest garments in a variety of African countries are imported from Europe, places such as Holland, Belgium, and England. The printed patterns are within the African aesthetic since the patterns and color combinations are developed by African expatriates living in these countries. Nonetheless, the production of these fabrics is carried out in far removed locations, usually because of the available technology and the economics of mass production.

The continental African based textile industry is in the developmental stages. It is possible that in the not too distant future, the textile industry used to create the fabrics and patterns desired by Africans and others interested in these materials will reside in the African countries themselves. With practical concerns of durability and availability aside, African-Americans would like to believe that fabrics and materials used to produce the garments worn in African-American performances originated in Africa.

For general costuming, there are a few contemporary materials which are being used as substitutes for natural or indigenous substances. These substitutes are available in Africa and the United States. For instance, yarn threads have almost completely replaced natural wool and animal hair as a material for decoration. The availability of vibrant colors and quantities on demand have dramatically changed the approach to costume building. These substitute materials can be shaped to allude to the original shapes and substances without the cost in money or man-hours needed to prepare and maintain performance clothing.

Part of this revolution in materials stems from a global awareness and the efforts of African countries to integrate with mainstream world culture. Colors that were never seen in the natural environment or the basic textile dying practices have caused more than a casual interest in colors and dyes available outside of continental Africa. Diarra discusses many of his observations made during his study with the national dance company of Mali:

> Well, you have to remember that most of the dyes that were used were from the ground, or from herbs. The colors were not as bright, so we get into synthetic things now, polyester, cotton, and rayon, and a lot of colors have just been created, like neons. What are those things?

> The first company from Mali went to Paris and saw all of these lights, and stages, and said, oh no, there's no way we can do this. We'd have to change the costumes, we'd have to change the colors. They believed they would have to change all of those things that they were traditionally using. Most of the Senoufo clothing was a mud print, it was very dark, and whatever white was in it was be-cause it was left there from the original color of the cloth. There was nothing like mirrors, and all that kind of stuff which didn't come into play until much later on.

> A lot of the things that we wear now, or even that they wear in Africa now that used to be raffia have been replaced with plastic bags. The burlap sacks used to hold imported food stuffs are plastic sacks now. The burlap sacks they used to unravel to make raffia skirts and head pieces are made from plastic. Raffia has, in a lot of places, been replaced by something else. Before, when raffia was used, it was the bark off the tree and herbs beat down to make it. A lot of those things now are being replaced, and a lot of raffia is being dyed all kinds of colors from purple to gray which makes it beautiful because it adds another whole dimension.

Symbolism

Within African culture, there are many objects, implements, colors, designs, articles of clothing, fetishes, and more that can be viewed in terms of their symbolic meaning with the peoples to whom they belong. Our concern is understanding which articles or elements are viewed as symbolic to African-Americans, or carry the same meaning in the United States as they do in Africa, or, how this symbolism is translated by African-Americans. The concepts and beliefs surrounding these articles are important to aesthetic thought.

We should first consider Africa itself, and the belief in a physical connection to the land and its people by African-Americans. Those people involved in the music and dance of Africa have acknowledged their kinship and familial ties to African culture through these activities. Sympathy for political, social, and economic conditions exist but for many African-Americans involved in the performance arts, financial resources are limited. Efforts to effect change in Africa by many African-Americans can only be made through advocacy and the support of political forces. The problem in attempting this recourse in the African-American community is the scarcity of information about these options and methods. Many African-Americans are still working to improve political, social, and economic conditions for themselves.

The music and dance of Africa are symbolic to many African-Americans. For many, they contain cultural information, beliefs, and lifestyle examples that should be part of African-American existence. To this end, meaning is sought in every aspect of African performance tradition seen in the United States. Viewers, students, and performers constantly ask for the cultural interpretations relevant to performance and costume. It is possible to have a literal interpretation and direct meaning in certain genres of African dance; those dances that recount history or other storytelling dances for example. Social dances may not have a clearly defined interpretation. In explanations offered for Mandiani, it is a social dance and does not tell a story. There are however more general interpretations that can and have been imposed on the movements of the dance. We would have to consider each possible interpretation in reference to the occasions or circumstances under which Mandiani was performed in past and present Africa. One general statement made is that Mandiani is the dance of the panther.

Dance and Symbolism

Symbolism adds another dimension to choreography. The primary concern expressed by American choreographers is for visibility from the audience. The general dance formation is second to that concern. According to Asante, block, circle, and line formations are typical in African dance. Deal discusses many aspects of the dance Mandiani, including choreographic setting:

> . . . (the formations used for the dance are) poly-geometric. When I
> say polygeometric, I mean out of a polygeometric perspective.
> Circles, lines, or parallel lines are two major formations, or a single
> line and/or a circle. Those geometric shapes are symbolic within
> the dance's meaning. For instance, the circle represents eternity and
> in initiation it represents the untouched eternity, meaning the un-
> touched infinity, the female genitalia, untouched in the circle. When
> a single line or two parallel lines are used and they cross, the cross-
> ing is symbolic of crossing over, the child going into adulthood. The
> line both parallel and singular is used as the symbol of crossing
> over because within that you have groupings that interchange. That
> is traditional choreography for initiation dances, not (set) in stone if
> you will, but it seems to be the preferred, and also symbolizing vir-
> ginity.

It is an acceptable assumption that movements and postures used in the work effort reveal themselves in cultural dance styles. According to a fact sheet distributed by the Sénégal Tourist Office, seventy-seven per- cent of Sénégal's labor force is in agriculture. There are several dance movements which reflect agricultural posture, the body bent forward at the waist and very low with scooping or harvesting arm and hand movements. We would expect to see these movement styles in the dance of an agricultural community. There are broad flinging motions that resemble those used by a fisherman casting a net. The people of coastal communities might use these motions in Mandiani.

Movement styles may be derived from natural elements and animals in their natural environment, especially those animals impor- tant to the community's lifestyle. Using this approach we would do best to observe lifestyles and examine how people go about their daily lives to look for other interpretations of these dance movements. Dancer Chuck Davis offers many of these analogies in the documentary, *Chuck Davis, Dancing Through West Africa*.[28] If historically the dance was seen as part of the progression toward the state of spirit possession, the wild or uncontrolled nature exhibited in several Mandiani movements might be understood in that context. In West Africa, the movements of Man- diani could symbolize this or other contextual interpretations. In the United States, very little from the African context exists. The only clear symbolic meaning carried from Africa by Mandiani in the United States was stated simply by Bayo and Konte when they said, "Mandiani is a happiness dance."

Drumming and Symbolism

The drum and the aura which surrounds it has many meanings. To the player, it is an instrument of fun and pleasure as well as a symbol of strength and power. Whether or not the lead drummer believes he or she is in the dominant position of the ensemble, the lead player carries that responsibility in class and performance situations. The political structure of the drum ensemble is that of a monarchy. Drum ensembles may be restricted in numbers because of the musical necessity for this hierarchy. Certain personality traits prevalent in the human male population, and certainly in the African-American male population make this reality a greater problem than one might hope. In considering the relatively powerless position of the average African-American male in the United States, it is reasonable to consider the drum ensemble as an environment where one person might exercise control over people and circumstances impossible to realize in other life situations.

In the past few years, there has been much research on the state of the African-American male. The drum ensemble provides for many a socially acceptable forum and outlet for the constructive release of tension. The accompanying psychological conditions and the use of the drum ensemble as a means of coping with these pressures should not be attributed or limited to African-American males. It is a natural human condition to want control over one's environment. Socialization promotes the controlled management of these tendencies.

The organization of the drum ensemble or group hierarchy has been related symbolically to African traditional village life and African family structure. The djimbe drum, itself, is said to symbolically represent village life. The center of the drum represents the chief, his quarters and other principals of the village. Moving outward from the center, the next area represents the villagers, then the fields, and finally, the area closest to the edge represents the waste. Other symbolism attached to the djimbe suggests that the entire drum is the symbol of human existence, the male represented by the shell of the drum, and the female represented by the drumhead. Oddly enough and in spite of the male and female representation in the total meaning of the drum, there are drummers in the United States who believe the djimbe should not be touched or played by women.

Several drummers have offered explanations of the male and female symbolism surrounding the djimbe. According to Chief Bey, one of the early drummers in the New York African drumming scene, the drum has both a male and female orientation. The wood shell represents the male factor and the animal skin which is placed over the wide end of the drum represents the female. The idea of interdependence and the belief that the drum is not whole without both parts is a concept found in many societies. However, the belief held by a few drummers is that the djimbe should not be played by females.

The notion that women should not play drums has been challenged. There are examples from the contemporary Mande culture that show women drumming. One of Dakar's revered drummers, Doudou Ndiaye Rose has shown this to the world. Other instances of females drumming have been observed in Sénégal with those females born into drumming families.

There are occasions during which access to drums is limited to specific personnel. These instances may be linked to occupational, caste, or political association. Spiritual or metaphysical beliefs might also restrict the number or gender of people permitted access to an instrument. One drummer in New York City was vehemently opposed to allowing another individual to handle his drum. The explanation given was that his drum had been blessed and medicines placed in the drum for him. If anyone else handled the instrument, the power of the blessing would be negated. A Sénégalese drummer stated that if the drumhead was cut by someone with a knife the gris gris or protection for the drummer and drum would be cancelled. This and other extreme instances of drum sanctification for select individuals can elevate the instrument to an untouchable status. The practicality of this protective viewpoint is obvious. At many times, the drum is vulnerable to damage, primarily to the skin. Protecting the drum may save replacing the drumhead prematurely. To abstain from approaching another musician's instrument without permission also reflects a point of common courtesy.

Drummers in the Mande cultures wear much of the protection required for drumming on their body or on their drum. Articles of clothing regarded as decorative may also be considered part of the belief system followed by musicians. A Ghanaian drummer/dancer pointed out scars on his body where protection had been placed just beneath his skin. The regular use of herbs, fetishes, or talismans for protection from ill wishers and for medicine does not occur or is not discussed by drummers and dancers in the United States. One artist did briefly address a few of these objects but asked that they not be brought to public attention. For him these herbs, fetishes, and talismans are sacred items used in his priestly role and responsibility to his community. It is possible to say that the power of the mind can create a reality from seemingly impossible circumstances if one believes these things are possible. [29]

The hair of certain animals and mirrors have symbolic meaning but may not be comprehended in the African-American aesthetic. The hair used on the hats worn by the djimbe players is expected to endow that player with the speed, power, and other desirable characteristics of the animal from which it was taken. Animal symbolism is represented in both the stance and the head gestures of the djimbe player. The posture of the proud cock with chest out or the fiercely heralded lion which is accompanied by symbolic rolls played on the djimbe exemplify this characteristic in Guinea djimbe playing, according to Bradley Simmons. According to Thiam, the head gestures of the djimbe player serve the utilitarian function of marking the beats much like a conductor uses a baton. Mirrors and other reflective decoration are used in the assembly of costumes in Africa and the United States. Diarra explains that the mirror is used to represent water and its purifying properties; the mirror concept is also used in the geometric designs created in fabric and costume patterns:

> A lot of mirrors in Africa are used to symbolize water. You have the triangle and the diamond shape. The line in the center creates that reflected image, the mirror image from the top to the bottom signifying the top and the bottom, the real world and the spiritual world. That concept was used through the spiritualism associated with the natural element itself, from the water, and applied to what was happening (being created). And then glass was brought to Africa along with new people moving and trading. African dance imitates and articulates the environment. So a lot of these (new) things were incorporated into the costume to show that reality such as beads and mirrors.

Color and Symbolism

Color symbolism in religious and social rituals has been a commonly discussed topic in many cultures. With African-Americans, there have always been lighthearted comments made to and about individuals who are attracted to bright colors and vibrant patterns, particularly the color red. Many folkloric cultures world-wide have examples of bright and vibrant color associations. The African disposition to combine diverse patterns in clothing was equated to their affinity for complex

Figure 3.7
Two Boys Dressed in White after the Circumcision Ceremony.

polyrhythms. Vibrating frequencies in bright colors and patterns are combined in unusual ways.

In my discussions with Diarra, Deal, and drummers and dancers in Sénégal there were two specific references to color. White seems to be associated with many events at, or for which Mandiani might be danced in Africa. One example cited described a pre-wedding celebration. All of the women in attendance wore white and those women representing the bride and groom were distinguishable by yellow ribbons. When young men return home from the circumcision ritual, white is worn. The boys wear loosely fitting white smocks and white skull caps which cover the entire head. Only the face and hands are seen. An example is shown in *Figure 3.7*. White is also the sign of mourning in many African societies.

Red is another color included in the discussion on symbolism and symbolic meaning. This color is commonly used in staged presentations by both African and African-American performing groups. When red is used for the color of cloth carried during certain rituals for example, consummating a marriage or after circumcision rites, the color represents blood. According to Diarra,

> The red fabric held during the dances or held in their hands was not painted red, it was the blood from the female to show that now she was ready to move from one stage of her life to another, or (it was used to show) . . . she (had) made (first) union with her husband. That cloth had to be there to prove she was a virgin. A lot of cloth held or displayed by male dancers was symbolic of the union between a female and themselves because that cloth was given to the male.

Color is a consideration for African-American performers. Many participants in dance classes arrive wearing what might appear to be a carefully planned orchestration of color and clothing design, often representing a mix of the traditional items, the seurre and moussr, with stylish contemporary colors and fabrics. Many of the dancers who attend African dance classes are uninhibited and free spirits. Their flair for style and eye catching colors seems consistent with the flamboyant character of Mande dance. Still, other individuals present a more pensive or studied approach to the dance, culture, and style. This is true for audiences as well as performers. Among the participants in Mande style dance, it is difficult to find individuals who simply want to "blend in." The overt qualities embodied by many participants are reflected in the colors and clothing they wear to informal gatherings. Concert attire for performers is somewhat different because the clothing worn in these situations is usually an culturally arbitrated decision by people other than the collective performers. The choices in costume, color, and fabric are made according to that which is perceived as authentic, but also what the viewer will accept as authentic and aesthetically pleasing. Symbolic representations may never enter the decision making process.

Cosmetics

An individual's physical appearance is one of the foremost culture based aesthetic considerations and should be addressed in the scope of African-American aesthetics. Mass communication has reached many formerly remote corners of the globe and certain cosmetic images, if not expectations, are developing at an ever increasing rate. The unique environment in the United States has western values which contribute to shaping this aesthetic. In the theatrical realm, Eurocentric concepts and

Figure 3.8
"Diam" — A Woman's Darkened Lower Face, Sénégal.

Figure 3.9
A Woman's Painted Hands in Sénégal.

interpretations are often imposed on the staged performance of African music and dance as a standard for these performances. Regardless of the theme, make-up and hair styling are two of the areas considered with a critical eye by the media, if not by select members of the audience and performers as well.

Two styles of body adornment are very foreign to western culture as practiced in several African countries; painting the hands and feet, and scarification. Scarification involves carving figures or designs into the skin and allowing them to heal, creating a permanent design. Another process requires puncturing the skin in a specific pattern and implanting a substance like charcoal much like a tattoo. Among traditional Moslem women, painting the hands and feet with henna is a common practice.[30] *Figure 3.8* is an example of facial darkening from Dakar. *Figure 3.9* shows one example of hand painting used by a woman in Ziguinchor, Sénégal. For African women who adhere to traditional practices, darkening the area around the mouth was considered an appropriate cosmetic treatment. Another option used by Sénégalese women is to prepare a cosmetic mask from henna. This is worn briefly before going out and "it gives you a good color."[31] In contemporary Africa among younger women this practice has been abandoned for western cosmetics although there may still be a few minor variations in the way they use them.

Decisions will always be made in accepting what is African reality and what is necessary in the United States cultural environment. Those herbs, oils, potions, and other substances used in traditional African practices or ritual may not be acceptable in the western environment. Concepts in Christian morality impose limitations on acceptable clothing, medical, and spiritual practices that in other societies might be accepted as normal. Examples might be the Rastafarian's use of marijuana or the Native American's use of peyote as part of their religious practices. These and other accepted practices in indigenous cultures contribute to the authenticity or certainly the reality of their culture.

What, if any, are the culturally accepted substances that contribute to the reality of Mandiani? Melvin Deal suggested that if the true substances used in the African setting for ritual were used in the United States, one might understand why the dance has such a wild and unrestricted abandon. One such substance he believed to be "cam," a white powder, is used on the skin of initiates as part of their preparation for the ceremony welcoming them to the adult community. American performers may know a powder is used but may not fully understand what that substance is and the effect it has on the wearer. Deal explains,

> They don't realize that cam is used during initiation because it is an anesthetic. I used this information in a lecture I called 'Earth and Drugs Yesterday and Today.' Cam provides a mysterious feeling which is part of the initiation experience. Initiation is supposed to be one of the most mysterious experiences that you ever have in your life above and beyond your first sexual experience. They smear cam on the initiates and that cam anesthetizes all the skin it touches, so that the face is anesthetized, they put it here (lower torso) it is anesthetized, if they put it from the knee down, that's anesthetized. Your body is in a semi-state of anesthetization when you dance.

Other cosmetic treatments found in the culture would probably not be acceptable in the United States because they can often be substitutes for clothing. In explaining this approach, Diarra stated, "They (the women) used to put powder, you know the lime or chalk, around them instead of panties and put on the seurre, and they would dance."

Styles for Women

The options chosen by African-Americans for staged performances are usually regulated by norms in the western aesthetic and in some instances, imposed by law. There are areas in the United States that restrict topless performance under local laws on obscenity or indecency. Other performance venues restrict the topless option, not because of legal constraints but in sympathy with conservative attitudes present among their patronage. There are African-Americans who have no objection to performing African dance topless or who have only minimal reservations. However, these individuals do not represent the total community. Regardless of what the legal system may or may not allow, many of the individuals involved with African dance are conservative in their personal point of view. Although African-American performers may not dispute the reality of topless performance in the African aesthetic, they make their decisions within the limits of acceptable and responsible behavior in the general community. Their willingness to perform in the rural tradition of Africa is limited by their personally defined conditions of audience, venue, and the concert producer's commitment to art and culture.

Another factor that serves to limit the possible costume and cosmetic options for African-American performers is the attention given to the definition of a desirable physical appearance for men and women in the western culture aesthetic. This volatile concept has changed many times over a number of years. The aesthetic views on physical and physiological appearance will follow what is generally achievable by the people who abide by that aesthetic. In the United States, the concepts defining beauty have traditionally been regulated by Eurocentric philosophies. There are people with vastly different body types attempting to define their own desirable characteristics, for example, senior citizens, full figured individuals, and balding men. The effort required by people of African descent to conform to Eurocentric views of beauty is in some instances very hard work and for others, impossible without medical or cosmetic surgery.

Today the western aesthetic describes a thin or slight physical structure as most desirable. This, in terms of physical appearance, is possible for many African-Americans but not for a vast majority. Anatomic characteristics of Africans and their descendants often display features such as fully developed buttocks, wide hips, thick lips, thick kinky hair, and broad noses and are in direct opposition to Caucasian physiology. Much of the costuming in African culture accentuates the more salient features of the native African. Among the Mande cultures, French colonial style garments are worn as well as traditional clothing and accessories for this very reason. For African women, these items can either accentuate the parts of the body that are important in African culture or obscure them.

The clothing options selected for most women in African-American performing groups include the marinier, halter top, or cowrie shell covered bra. The garments selected for the lower body include the seurre, the belefeté, or the thiaya (pants). The final decisions are often made based on personal comfort but not always concern for the original context of the dance. In discussing these options with dancers, the double seurre and long seurre are the least desirable for performance due to the problems presented restricting movement, but they are acceptable. The thiaya, as an option, allows the male or female dancer to perform movements in a very free and comfortable manner that might not be comfortable in other clothing styles because of modesty.

Styles for Men

The clothing used to dress men in the performing ensemble is determined according to the application: the dancer, or the musician. They are usually considered separately and the choice is related to the frequency of exits and returns to the stage made by the dancer, and the necessity for musicians to remain on stage for long periods of time. The decisions therefore take into account the flexibility or nondescript appearance for the musicians. These performers may play continuously through a variety of dances which represent several dance styles and cultures. Dancers find it desirable to change their costume to better reflect the culture represented in the dance being performed.

Drummers, particularly those representing the Mande cultures, have a fairly simple existence in this area. Clothing for the djimbe player is well defined. According to all of the informants interviewed, the basic item worn by the djimbe player is the hat. The height and shape of the headpiece may vary six to twelve inches or more in elevation from the top of the performer's head to the top of the headpiece. Animal hair, particularly that of the horse and cow, is often used to adorn the headwear. Many of the hats worn by drummers are designed with a crescent shape arching from the front of the forehead to the nape of the neck. The hat is part of the clothing worn by Mandingo warriors. To date, little is known in the United States, in concrete terms, about the origins of its shape. It was suggested that this particular headpiece might have developed after seeing helmets worn by the Portuguese and other early European explorers.[32] Regardless of the specific origins, it is the expected head wear for djimbe players in many of today's cultures.

Another article of clothing associated with the Mandingo warrior is raffia worn around the waist. In contemporary costuming practices this material is created by unraveling burlap fabric panels and twisting a few strands at a time together, or unravelling woven plastic panels. The natural grass-like material is still available and used in both Africa and the United States but the convenience of alternative substances is often preferable to traditional substances. Drummers can wear raffia, however, in the United States it is a principal costuming material for dancers. Drummers and dancers usually wear the thiaya. These pants were said to have been brought to sub-Saharan Africa by the Arabs.

Male drummers in the United States usually appear in chest pieces or the rectangular top. The topless option is used from time to time by drummers but is most often seen with male dancers. There has not been any definitive reason given for the choice made by drummers. Costumers still seem to prefer to have the drummer in a top, as opposed to no top at all, possibly reflecting that same sense of modesty expressed earlier. Diun diun players usually appear in similar dress to the djimbe

Figure 3.10
Examples of Carving on Drum Tails.

players without the hat. On their heads is usually a headband or nothing at all. Female drummers generally conform to the costuming of female dancers, usually wearing the greater rather than the lesser amount of clothing. Dancers are obliged to dress as close to the style of the region represented in the dance being performed as possible.

Costumes are a significant concern with presentations in the United States. When possible, it is desirable for the performers to use several different costume changes. These changes will usually offer a variety of design, color, and style combinations for each dance, if possible. For both women and men, these costume changes aid in projecting the meaning and significance of the dance being presented or at least that each dance is perceived differently.

Instruments

Djimbe players in the United States are generally interested in the shape, size and appearance of the instrument. The look of the drum is always more aesthetically appealing if a decorative pattern has been carved on the drum. *Figure 3.10* shows examples of carving on two different djimbes. There are many drums in the United States that have a design on the tail or pipe similar to example "A." As the owners of these drums encounter each other, there is a feeling of association almost as if one has found a relative who was previously unknown to them. From the available information, this design originated in Sénégal and may have been done by the same carver. View "B" is an example of an elaborately carved drum. View "C" was carved by Yacine Gueye and he claims his symbol to be the continent of Africa. Other United States drummers have taken it upon themselves to carve their own drums with symbols meaningful to them. A few drums found in the United States have very elaborate carving on the tail or the body of the instrument as seen in view "D." This decorative covering is always appealing and desired. It is rare, however, that any individual interested in purchasing an instrument has the option of selecting from a variety of instruments in the same place. Therefore, the choice of purchasing a drum that is carved or uncarved may not be available. More often, it is only over a period of time and the ownership of several instruments that a drummer finds an instrument that meets all of the aesthetic criteria. Before the criteria on size, weight, color, sound properties, and cosmetic appearance are met, a drummer may buy and sell several instruments. In addition, it is rare that a drummer finds one instrument which satisfies all of the criteria. Most players will find themselves owning several instruments at a time and designating each drum for certain situations or playing applications.

One of the most aesthetically gratifying or frustrating processes associated with drum ownership is that of replacing a drum head. The process is rather involved, and many players would rather not do the work themselves. Even so, drummers will have specific guidelines for how they would prefer the instrument to look at the end of the process. The original method in Africa involved fitting the animal skin around a ring made from natural fibers. To attach the skin to the drum, holes were used around the edge of the skin to anchor the cord. Ahmed spoke of the djimbe drum he first saw Ladji Camara use when he was Camara's student in New York City:

> When I first saw Ladji's drum, it was tied with a couple of different kinds of cord, telephone wire, and lacing went all directions. That was the way it was. He didn't care about what it looked like. Over there (Africa) they used whatever was available.

Other contemporary drummers from Sierra Leone and Côte D'-Ivoire have used similar utilitarian approaches to lacing the djimbe. Ahmed commented that in preparing his own drum, little attention is paid to the symmetry or color of the cord. However, if he is replacing a drumhead for someone else, care is taken to assure symmetrical horizontal and vertical laces. Care must be taken in the initial preparation and positioning of the top and bottom rings which provide the anchoring points for the vertical lace. "Chief Bey was the first to use metal rings on a drum. Little by little, the drums that came over started to have metal rings on them."[33] Some players prefer a cord nesting ring attached to the metal ring while others prefer to tie directly to the metal rings. "This gives you a tighter pull because it's more direct" (Simmons 1990). The system which does not use a nesting ring is difficult to work with. Those who prefer the cord nesting ring can be assured of evenly placed loops and a symmetrical net pattern. For many, this visual presentation of the drum is an aesthetic priority.

There are players who believe it is aesthetically pleasing to have articles attached to the drum. Drums have been observed with beaded strands or belts, strips of kinte cloth, or strings of bells attached to them. The kesingkesings are likely to be etched by players. These decorative items, according to the players who use them, are symbolic. When asked if there are ever items used on the drum for decoration other than the kesingkesings in Sénégal, Gueye replied, "There is medicine for the drum and the drummer, but it is put inside the drum." Another aesthetic treatment found in preparing the drum is in leaving the hair on that portion of the drumhead that sits below the playing surface of the instrument. This collar has not been observed to any great extent on the drums of older players from Sénégal, Guinea, Mali, or the United States. In fact, veterans normally do not leave an excessive amount of hide beyond what is necessary to secure the skin to the drum shell. Nonetheless, instruments observed entering the country recently have retained this hairy collar and it seems to be most attractive to younger generations of players and observers.

The djimbe is usually the drum that attracts people to the drum ensemble, but the diun diun is often assigned to players as their introduction to the drum ensemble, and rightfully so, according to most of the djimbe players interviewed. It is also the drum that should be listened to for rhythms by most American dancers. The diun diun is important for giving the dance rhythm, basic time, and pulse according to the

African dancers. The importance of this instrument should not be understated but often is. Those American drummers cognizant of the role played by the instrument believe the diun diun carries the same aesthetic significance and importance as the djimbe. The same concerns for size and decorative treatment, including color, and the physical properties such as weight and sound are significant to the players of this instrument although the diun diun is usually lowest in priority when drummers choose an instrument to play.

Size may be the most significant factor in the overall attraction to the diun diun because it is directly related to the pitch range attainable. If the drum is large, the drum is expected to have a low sound. The drums in the United States, as well as Africa, are now usually made from industrial steel drums, the same drums used to store or transport dry or liquid industrial materials. The average size appears to be a twenty gallon steel drum, approximately fourteen inches in diameter and twenty inches long. With this size can, the drum can be tuned to a reasonably low pitch. An option used by several of the diun diun players very committed to creating a drum with an exceptionally low and resonant sound was the thirty gallon can. This size will produce a thunderous sound, but it is more difficult to carry in the traditional manner. True devotes will find a fifty gallon drum. One of the instruments used by the Guinea Ballet was such a drum; however, it was played in a stationary position, and not carried by the player.

The weight of the drum is partially linked to the materials used in its construction. The steel drum, for its size, is relatively light. Wood is the traditional material used to build the diun diun in Africa. A wood instrument is not usually as large as the steel drums because of the weight. The sound of a wood drum, to many, is the only acceptable sound. In describing the sound, words such as warm, round, and deep are often used. Among contemporary players in Africa and the United States, the steel can is a common option, and it is readily available.

Color is another consideration in the construction of the drum. This cosmetic consideration seems much more prevalent among American diun diun players than their African counterparts. Two possible explanations can be suggested. If the drum is made of wood, the feeling may be there is little need for further alteration because this natural material, in itself, is aesthetically pleasing. If a metal drum is used, many African-American drummers find it important to cosmetically transform the instrument from a bland, industrial colored exterior to conform to other color schemes and aesthetic values held by the individuals. In many instances, these metal drums can be obtained already painted but with few color options. Few players are satisfied with whatever the existing color might be. Others have given their instrument a distinctive identity by repainting the drum or covering the shell with fabric or animal skins.

Since the system used to attach the drumhead to the diun diun is the same as that used to attach the drumhead to the djimbe, cosmetic control over the geometric shapes created in the tying process and choice of cord color are also possible. Although there is a large amount of open space on the diun diun, players seem to limit their effort to decorate the instrument to previously discussed surface treatments. Occasionally, other sonic devices such as beads, jingling rings, or small bells which do not provide a specific rhythm part, fabrics and fetishes have been used to adorn drums in the United States.

Theatrical Properties and Accessories

The mask is one of the items regularly associated with African dance. Many of the artifacts looked upon as statues and typically disassociated with performance are, in fact, carried over the head, or they may cover the face, entire head, or a major portion of the body. All of these articles that are used in that way should be viewed as masks. The Egungun is one of the more familiar masked dances seen in the United States.[34] In theatrical productions, masks are said to represent a variety of deities, seasons, rites, spirits, and more. There are very few authorities in the United States to ask about the Mande cultural use of masks in dances readily accessible to the African-American community. Nor is there is a great body of information available through written sources. Olatunji was the first African performer accessible to the Black community through his institute in New York City. Many of the spin-off groups copied Olatunji's repertoire, including his masked dance.

> Well in the early sixties, it wasn't which ones (cultures) attracted
> you, it was the ones that you had access to. Yoruba was, of course,
> primary because Olatunji's performances, although what he was
> portraying in his dance music was not strictly the Yoruba tradition,
> the singing and etc., were Yoruba based. So, you found that out of
> the Olatunji genre if you will, came a plethora of little Olatunji
> groups all over the country. Many did not survive and many did.
> And I can admit that our repertoire was identical to Olatunji's. We
> did Odunde, we did quote, unquote, 'The Mask Dance' untitled. It

> was just raffia and a mask, and it was called The Mask Dance. We
> had no concept of the role of the mask, in the traditional society.
> They did a mask dance called The Mask Dance, so every group had
> a 'The Mask Dance.'

There are very few masked dances performed by African-American groups, and of these dances performed, there are only a few identified as Mande. One story heard and seen in the United States from the Mande region is Kaki Lambe, an epic tale told through dance. Kaki Lambe is a god said to possess the power to grant good luck, health, and prosperity for one year at a time. Saa is a dance said to have been created by Ladji Camara, after coming to the United States, to portray one of the many legends of his people. Saa was a bird creature that was called upon to save the youth of a Senoufo village after they built a huge ship and filled it with gold to sail off and show the world all of their riches. Other masks used in the United States are the Nimba, a fertility figure, and the Shiwarra, an antelope figure also representing fertility. In these presentations, the mask is used in themes of agriculture and childbearing. Aziz Ahmed explained the function of the mask by saying, "The dancer does not wear the mask to dance, the individual is dancing the mask." The understanding is that the dancer is not really in control of what will happen after donning the mask. Deal has also been interested in masked dances for some time. He explains,

> The masquerade is either for a secret society, entertainment, or
> both. I've always had an interest in masquerades, the Igunno-ko
> and masquerades of that nature. For a while, I've been involved in
> the study of the purpose for the masquerade in traditional society.
> I've done, oh, about five or six masquerades in our repertoire.
> We've done Egungun, Igunno-ko, Gélédé from Nigeria, Kumpo
> from Sénégal and then of late, we've done the Dan entertainment
> mask which is our most recent projection. Bobo, yes, some Bobo
> masks of Upper Volta also. Many of the companies that dance here
> (in the United States) don't do masquerade. It's strictly dance (for
> them) and I think one reason for that is that masquerades are not
> bombastic enough. They're not kinetically wowing enough. Groups
> are not realizing that one of the greater projections of dance and
> music is the masquerade. The masquerade is very important.

There have been productions by Black dance and theater companies that have used African styled masks. If a mask is created for theatrical reasons, the creators do not expect their creation to have any mystical powers. If, however, the mask is from a particular identifiable culture, African-American participants are more cautious and less inclined to get involved with an object that might have great or dire consequences if used improperly, or if they are required to portray rituals that are represented as authentic acts. An example of this caution was seen in the preparation for a performance at the Los Angeles Theater Center with Olatunji's performing company in 1986. In this presentation, Olatunji was attempting to recreate on stage a vignette of African life from his childhood memories. One of the scenes involved a young couple who had been unsuccessful in their efforts to have a child. They visited a person knowledgeable in herbs, medicines, and the proper spirits required to remove the obstacles blocking this important responsibility in the African sensibility. Certain rites were performed and a song was sung to Kori, goddess of fertility. The members present at this particular rehearsal had been performing with Olatunji for some time, and none of them were willing to represent the young married couple in this staging because almost all of the ritual was included, and they were not willing to risk the projected outcome. At another rehearsal, one couple did agree to become the people in the vignette. Interestingly enough, the women who took part in the production became pregnant in less than six months after the performance. This may easily have been coincidental, but all of the members of Olatunji's group firmly believed the pregnancy was the direct result of the woman's involvement with the fertility ritual. There are many African-Americans who hold great respect for rituals and beliefs based on their African and African-American past.

Rarely are idols, statues, or other fetishes used in African-American productions of African dance and there is no evidence of a mask for the dance Mandiani. There is caution used in the selection of material chosen for performance. Concern is taken not to evoke some unknown power, a thought that is real to many involved in African music and dance. There are many myths and stories surrounding African culture that continue to contribute to the mystery of Africa for African-Americans. Belief in the supernatural, and misconceptions about Africa are present in the non-performing community as well.

In December of 1991, during a Kwanzaa celebration concert in Phoenix, Arizona, a father told his young son that the women seated on stage were the wives of the only male involved in that particular part of the performance. The father clearly believed this to be true because polygamy is the lifestyle in Africa, as he understands it. This was not true for the performance and in contemporary Sénégalese culture many men have chosen to have only one wife. This father's perception of this staged event and his assumptions about Africa serve to illustrate that these myths, stories, and legends still form the greater part of misinformation prevalent in the general African-American community.

In the staging of African dance performances, there is a strong desire to have foliage and other stage settings which suggest an African village. Often, the problem is finding or creating the appropriate objects to match the music and/or setting in which the music and dance would naturally take place. The major touring companies from Africa are able to prepare and hang painted backdrops and scenery that is suggestive of a region or environment in which some portion of the performance might take place. It is extremely costly and not very practical to travel with the variety of articles and stage props needed to represent all of the music and dance properly, even for the largest national groups.

Smaller performing groups encounter economic problems in acquiring stage sets, transporting them, and storage when they are not in use. Even if a community based organization has the financial means to create a substantial stage set, repeated use might create the unwanted impression among local followers that the set has been utilized many times; repeated use detracts from the material presented. Audience attention during a performance is generally focused on the performers. From a financial perspective, most performing groups in the United States have decided that resources are better used for articles worn or used in the performance of African music and dance rather than on stage sets and dressings. An effort is put forth during major performances to provide the essence of a scene or environment associated with the materials presented. Preparation for this aspect of performance is given a position of low priority because of financial considerations.

In comparison, accessories are given a great deal of attention. Since those articles carried or worn are typically questioned by curious audiences, efforts are made to present items and articles that support the theme of the performance piece. In this regard, the approach is often consistent with other western ideas for staged productions relevant to performer safety and ease in carrying out the projected task. For example, in the performance of a dance to Ogun, a Yoruba deity, the performer will probably use rubber or unsharpened axes or knives for the safety of the performer. Other objects worn such as bracelets, anklets, necklaces, beaded belts, and amulets are important accessories for women along with various styles of chest pieces, arm bands, and beaded strands for male dancers and drummers.

Many accessory items worn by performers have representations in the culture other than simple decoration or body adornment. Many of the items worn around the neck and arm are supposed to be vehicles or vessels for protective medicines in the culture. Among African-American ensembles, the attention is directed toward bright, colorful items; however, it is usually in the small and seemingly dull and uninteresting items that powerful or spiritual substances are contained for African cultures. For staged performances, there is continuity between the contemporary touring African groups and African-Americans in their attraction to colorful accessories. With musicians, there is greater attention given to accessories in the United States than with touring African companies. The basic costume for musicians may be more elaborate with touring African groups, and they are generally uniform throughout with a possible increase in adornments for the lead players. American groups often project a feeling of variety in the visual dimension for musicians but may also use costumes that are uniform in design.

In this chapter we have discussed material and tangible aspects of Mandiani as it has manifested itself in the African-American community. I have chosen the narrative style in order to portray the human experiences related to me, along with the data derived from the many conversations and observations that took place. By including observations and related items from African sources, the similarities between the two cultures were emphasized. The instruments, movements, songs and clothing have changed very little from their original forms and presentation. Context is the major difference between the two cultures and the presentation of Mandiani. Limited access to information by African-Americans is another. These factors have had an impact on the way Mandiani has been realized in the United States. In Chapter Four we will examine the thoughts and feelings that illustrate similarities and differences, beyond artifacts and tangible items. At the psychological level, concepts, ideas, beliefs and emotions address the heart and soul of the African-American aesthetic and those qualities which are related to a greater Black aesthetic.

Chapter Four

The Psychological Aesthetic

Symbolism, concepts of time, intelligence, emotion, and ego: these are concerns which are formulated in the mind and affect the individual psyche. These concerns are impacted by external elements and events but reside within the individual and affect thoughts, desires and motivations. Each has an effect on one's conception of self or how one is perceived by others. A culture's aesthetic will also include these concepts since the aesthetic view is derived through a social consensus of thoughts and beliefs.

Through earlier observations and discussions in this book, visible and conscious motivations which were part of the African-American aesthetic were examined as they related directly to Mandiani, and as they may reflect more universal ideas. There are personal and private thoughts that motivate individuals to participate in this activity. Intellectual gratification, the challenge to successfully reproduce this music and dance, and the thrill of conquering this challenge is expressed in the mind. Aspects of the aesthetic may be deeply seated in long standing cultural traits that link these two cultural realities, African and American, together on a more fundamental level. The concept of humanness is universal. In the human condition, there are many ideas common to all mankind. The following observations are specific to the African-American community and Mandiani but may also suggest common issues in many societies.

Dance is often viewed as therapeutic in requiring high degrees of mental concentration and physical commitment. According to the dancers, there is no place for other thoughts while performing. Mandiani music and dance liberates the mind and spirit from daily concerns. A respite from daily thought can, in itself, be beneficial. Because of the mental and physical commitment required for performance, there is a similar release offered to the musician. Djimbe drummers receive their gratification from two sources, the physical demands and the achieved volume. The commitment can be so complete that in some instances the performer has total disregard for personal conditions, in order to insure the inspired execution of the dance. Both dancers and drummers can appreciate the cathartic benefits of physical involvement.

Volume is identified as a stimulant by drummers and dancers in the United States and the Mande communities of West Africa. At the expected volume, it becomes impossible to focus on anything outside of the music sound. The biological byproduct of the resultant intense effort is the release of endorphins to the brain which have the effect of suppressing stress and anxiety. After completing such strenuous activity, the accompanying feeling of gratification is often enhanced by knowing that a multiplicity of objectives have also been reached in serving the community, the most important of which are education and entertainment. Personal gratification is derived from the physical connectedness to the culture. Dancers and drummers receive satisfaction from this visual display.

There is a collective sense of power experienced by dancers and drummers on an ensemble and personal level. This feeling is born from a sense of having control over one's environment. The need to conform to a general dance objective is balanced by the opportunity to express one's individuality through solos. For individuals who find comfort in performing in consort with others, music and dance activity provides this experience. For individuals who need to extend themselves beyond the group context, solo opportunities also exist.

Symbolism

The connection between African and African-American culture is recorded in global history, and genealogy presents clear evidence of that connection. In the reference by African-Americans and Africans to the African continent, the phrases "Africa," "The Mother Land," or, "Mother Africa," are at the very base of this symbolic reference. There are still several opinions presented to African-Americans by western and African culture that strain the basic understanding of this connection. The notion that African-Americans are Americans first, and that they would not be easily accepted in the eyes of Africans, has been promoted in the United States for many years. Recently, with the blossoming of Afrocentric thought, those ideas are continually being counteracted by African-Americans who have successfully made the pilgrimage to Africa. References to African brothers and sisters reinforce the family as a universal symbol connecting the two continents.

In Africa, visiting African-Americans must be prepared for the misconceptions held by many Africans about life and living in the United States. Although in several ways life may not be as difficult in the United States for African-Americans as it may be for many Africans in Africa, there are parallel difficulties in daily existence for many African-Americans. These ideas will be sorted out in time as more accurate information reaches both continents. Most of the individuals in the United States and Africa who share similar life conditions will probably never have the opportunity to observe these similarities for themselves. Presently, performances of African music and dance may provide the closest contact with African culture that many African-Americans will experience.

The encouragement given by elders to younger generations to pursue African culture, either passively or actively, reflects a commitment in aesthetic thought. Many African-Americans still view drum and dance activity from a western perspective. It must be understood that the African-American aesthetic also has an American component, and Afrocentric thought contains ideas that can be found in both African and European cultures. The intellect will allow an individual to focus on one area or the other; nonetheless, it would be very difficult to completely eliminate thoughts from either perspective which have existed and helped shape the Afrocentric position for generations. Music and dance is symbolic of an African concept held by African-Americans that is often intangible, resulting from the absence of substantive materials available through public education systems.

Viewing and performing African dance in America should also be considered entertainment for both viewer and performer. The sense of belonging to Africa and empathic sensations acquired through the observation of African music and dance are not reliant on a deep understanding of African culture, but rather on emotional and intellectual perceptions or cognitions gathered from the material presented. Finite movement and music components may be lost in the process of assimilation because the ability to absorb characteristic African music and movements is directly related to dance movements and music sounds that have been more resilient in popular African-American culture.

Familiar motor/movement and rhythmic patterns are more easily retained and reproduced. As long as there are contemporary African sources available, African-Americans will continue to absorb more details and nuances from the African culture bearers. We could still consider African-Americans in the same way as many of the Africans we encountered, that is, a part of the family which is now in a different place.

The principal focus of groups in the United States is on dance, and the overwhelming number of participants are female. Many of these women are leaders. This would suggest that in addition to organizational skills and interpersonal skills, these women have assumed the role of culture bearers in this country. This responsibility often falls to women in traditional societies as well. In African national touring companies, the representation of men and women is almost equal. Groups observed in Africa usually have male leadership. The reality of male dominated African societies should be tempered with the recognition of female contributions, which are often unsung.

A popular belief in the United States is that the drummer should control the dance presentation. Although this is often the case, it also happens that the drummer quite often responds or reacts to the dancer's movements. The drummer may inspire the dancer to elevated performance levels but a contrary perspective often realized by performers is that the dancer can also inspire the drummer to levels of creativity that are extraordinary.

The mysticism associated with body movements and gestures in the African culture does not always find its way into the explanations received by African-Americans. According to many of the principal informants for this study, these explanations are not often received because those questions are not asked or the answers are deemed to be protected and privileged information. In the execution of the music and movement, African-Americans look for meaning that is directly translatable or metaphoric. Part of the explanation for many of the gestures used in African dance is derived from context. Dance gestures can easily mimic everyday activities and are seen as such by members of the culture. The concept of crossing over, traversing the boundaries between childhood and adulthood has been long removed from the American culture in any formal way. There are, of course, equivalent benchmarks in the growth of American youth such as the first social date, the acquisition of a driver's license, and graduation from high school. These activities mark significant changes in the lives of young people, but they occur over many years, and adulthood is obtained in stages.

In traditional African societies, reaching adulthood happened all at once, and suddenly one became an adult. In recent years, various groups in the United States have attempted to include this coming of age or rite of passage ritual. In these groups, African dances, including Mandiani, are being incorporated into mainstream African-American culture and are used in an attempt to create components based in ritual and custom. The spiritual and mystical components may never be truly experienced here as they are on the African continent because of our need for scientific explanations.

The tangible items that are valued in the visual aesthetic have symbolic importance. Fabrics used in costuming can impart a sense of belonging to the greater African culture while being worn. The association with traditional patterns and colors is significant, but if this fabric can be said to have passed through the African continent, a much greater connection to Africa is felt. The colors red and white are found in the spiritual and ritual context in both African-American and African societies. Vibrating frequencies in light and sound impact our senses. Vibrant and eye catching colors are consistently found in Black communities. The use of designs and patterns that may not conform to the conventional western aesthetic has always been visible in African cultures. These designs and patterns are also quite prominent in the African-American community and accepted across all age groups. The vibrating frequencies present in bright colors and dramatic patterns printed on fabric is comparable to polyrhythmic drum textures. This parallel comparison to a variety of patterns and frequencies for the eye and the polyrhythmic nature of the drum music for the ears is thought by my African informants as one way they create and view their world. These people identify aesthetically with this collage of sight and sound. It then follows that those African-Americans who also identify with these perceptions are demonstrating their continuity with this sensual component of the Black aesthetic.

It is odd that for the African-American, the spiritual and mystic unknown are often missed in the understanding of costume, music, and dance. In costuming, to be eye catching or visually stimulating are not the justifications originally attached to many items. Mirrors, animal hair, fetishes, shells, and beads are acceptable as purely decorative items but there are deeper meanings. For musicians, the symbolism surrounding the music and the musicians may be more clearly understood, or at least introduced to a large number of participants who play the drums or wear the clothes. The symbolism surrounding the drum and the male/female relationship presented by it is not examined by many. In the male sphere, this understanding is sometimes twisted to serve individual interests rather than to support universal concepts in relationships.

Movements are studied by the way they are produced, and the techniques used, but not by what they symbolize. Masked dances are even less understood when performed in the United States. As a result, meaning is reduced to visual stimulation. There may be an alternative justification. A possibility for the exclusion of masked dances in the United States is their association with the unknown and the spirit world. Performers are unlikely to tamper with the unknown. The effect and true use of the music is also lost and it may end up simply accompanying the dance without communicating the power of music in the culture.

Time and Cultural Aesthetics

Time is an issue that has been related to cultures and cultural practices for generations. The importance of being on time in western culture is paramount. With many third world cultures and minority cultures in the United States, there are great disparities in the concept of time and the importance of time as viewed by western societies. In the African-American community there is a general consensus of opinion related to time which is apparent in interviews, classes, rehearsals, and performances. Unless there are very stringent time parameters placed on the use of a facility, events will invariably begin after the scheduled time. It is also the norm rather than the exception that one or more individuals will arrive even after the start of serious work. Dorothy Pennington articulated two time concepts in the piece entitled "Time in African Culture," mechanical and organic time. Nationalities and nations have reputations based on their interpretations of these time concepts.

Among African-Americans, time relative to scheduling appointments, the beginning and ending of events, the time required to prepare, initiate and conclude activities is a significant issue. Time and culture-related anecdote is often told. Though these axioms are usually grounded in fact, there is little thought given to the cultural ideology that may have led to these culture related concepts. In discussing time in African culture, Pennington said:

> . . . the more a group perceives itself as being in control of its fate and destiny, the more time-conscious it will be. On the other hand, those who perceive that there is a higher force in charge will likely be less time-conscious, reasoning that no matter how conscientiously humans plan their lives, they are not the final determinants of events.[1]

African-Americans have come from a deeply spiritual background and cultural experience which has taught them that no matter how difficult life is on earth, there is a better place waiting for them after death, and there is a higher power in charge of their destiny. Pennington's explanation of this African time concept is based on the importance of the past and present in African society. Continuity through time is established with a perspective from the past to the present, not projected from the present to the future. This is also a philosophy held in the African-American community. Time is related to a natural order and even though cyclicity in nature is inevitable, the variability of nature within the larger cycle forces one to minimize the importance of precise mechanical time. Yet, mechanical time is the norm in western culture.

In the African community "The concept of time is determined, among other things, by the religious and philosophical doctrines, by the view of the progression and links of existence, and by the nature of the activities engaged in at a particular time."[2] For social events within the African-American community, there is an understanding that the real excitement of the event does not begin until well into the designated time. There are also logistical problems such as transportation and family management which often delay the arrival of many participants. The religious belief that one's destiny is in the hands of God is a strong feature in African-American existence, and this belief has been expressed throughout history. Socially the belief that events and occasions will proceed with or without a particular individual present has come about because of the high number of variable conditions in African-American culture. Within the African-American community, this second approach may not be openly condoned, but it is accepted.

Classes and rehearsals represent elective activities, and they are prioritized as such. Punctuality is affected by other events in the daily life cycle ranging from business matters out of the individual's control, to fatigue and the decision as to which is more important at that time, attending an elective activity or rest. When there must be compliance with western time frames, controversies over the individual's approach to punctuality arise. These factors create a dichotomy within the combined cultures in the United States. In the aesthetic perception of African and African-Americans, "Time for traditional Africans (and many African-Americans) has been organic, rather than mechanical."[3]

Intelligence and Cultural Aesthetics

The way African-Americans learn Mandiani is couched in a cultural aesthetic based on a traditional learning approach used in African communities referred to as oral tradition. In contemporary society, data transmission is sometimes facilitated with the use of contemporary electronic technology, audio and video cassette tape, but even with this technology, information transferral retains this basic oral/aural approach. Although instruction in dance and music notation is available and could facilitate the learning process, that option is rarely taken. Learning develops through the senses of sight, sound, and movement.

Language has developed which is quickly understood for music instruction. In a few music and dance situations, individual instructors have successfully incorporated western approaches or developed their own interpretations of European instructional languages, and often come very close to the intended application. This is done to help those people caught in a word-oriented culture. This music and dance language is developed and sustained by performers and teachers within regional communities. Even though this language may have common elements with other regions, it is expected that it will also take on a regional individuality. As in language, it should be expected that each region will develop idiosyncratic characteristics which can be compared to the development of regional dialects in linguistic studies.

There is another manifestation of this intelligence which becomes highly developed through active participation in music and dance. This takes the form of dance progressions, sequences, and coded signals between participants. Communication is necessary during the act of performance and includes the interpretation of signals, both visual and verbal, remembered sequences of events and activities, the recognition of particular body movements that are specific to the individuals in signalling their intentions, and recognizing musical characteristics associated with individual drummers. All of this aids the interpretation of musical ideas. We look at these skills as being intuitive because of their non-verbal nature. Still, they are learned skills which have always been an important component in the performing arts for most cultures.

Ego and Cultural Aesthetics

Taking control of one's own destiny reflects ego. Belief in one's self and holding to one's convictions, determining what is good, bad, beautiful, desirable or undesirable is a function of one's own ideas. Ego is shaped in part by socialization, religious edicts, personal beliefs, and common practices as realized by the individual. All of these things can have a positive or negative impact on the formation of ideas. Decisions that are made to satisfy personal needs and desires, deciding on those things that bring pleasure, and all other decisions made so that one has control over one's own destiny are part of one's personal aesthetic. Common ideas, attitudes and approaches to problems among a few individuals may be coincidental. If, however, there are common concepts within a community, if there is consensus in the approach to these positions, a community aesthetic is formed.

The individuals involved with African drum and dance are usually very clear in their ideas and opinions concerning themselves and their community. They all have strong egos. Quite often each individual is a potential leader in his or her respective area of performance. The competitive spirit is obvious, and gives the music and dance vitality. After achieving the distinction of being a principal performer, the individual psyche is comforted through the experiences of personal independence in solos played and danced, the autonomous and yet integral relationship of one member to another, and the direct experience of interdependence in both music and dance. Dancers make efforts to reproduce individual movements and to be seen individually. The same is true of many drummers in their desire to present musically distinct and significant parts within the sound matrix. The desire is expressed by many drummers and dancers to be the designated soloist, and to exist for a brief period of time outside of the structured ensemble mosaic. The approach taken to secure these solo positions, or derive these experiences may not always be overt, and may not be done consciously by the individual. Nonetheless, these are factors in the creation, development, and production of African music and dance in the United States. These attitudes are components of the individual psyche found in the performing arts and it is logical to expect that intense physical demands require strong psychological postures. Mandiani and other Mande dances bring out this quality in each participant.

Within the ensemble, and along with the competitive spirit, there can exist an atmosphere of community. There is great pride taken in the material performed, and all of the presenters would like to believe that within the scope of African music and dance, they are being true to African culture. The opinions held by males on gender roles and male dominance have been based on ideas from earlier perceptions of Africa and Africans. These ideas are slow to be dismissed. Ideas projected by contemporary male drummers are now reflecting more liberal positions than in the past. New attitudes are emerging in the area of male/female relationships, and in attitudes toward the role of females in African and American society. Although the individual personalities comprising the ensemble are often very opinionated, there is an acceptable relinquishing of a portion of self for the success of the whole, and a collective attitude that is rather intolerant of those who are not willing to compromise.

Summary of Aesthetic Points Held by African-Americans Associated with Mandiani

One goal of this exploration is to identify an aesthetic that may be applicable to the African-American community at large, and to identify new elements or corroborate previous statements in the Black aesthetic. In using the narrative approach, a broad spectrum of ideas and concepts has been revealed about Africans and African-Americans and Mandiani. This is, admittedly, a small and specialized population, but as suggested previously, the individuals involved display characteristics of the larger African-American community.

Kwabena Nketia suggests there are two principal lines of inquiry in the pursuit of aesthetics theory, "aesthetics as 'sensuous cognition' and aesthetics as 'theory of work of art.' "[4] In the past, these two approaches often led to very different observations about similar material. This investigation has been pursued from an Afrocentric perspective in order to realize the relationship between both positions. In developing theories for aesthetic issues, we must look at what exists and attempt to make sense of it. Theories allow us to predict what might happen. Over time these theories will either prove to be true or not. Theories look to what might be true in the future. Sensuous cognitions look at what has happened from the past to the present. In this study of Mandiani, we have the opportunity to look at a music and dance activity which has significance in a historic sense, but is also relevant to contemporary Mande and African-American culture. Cognitions of the senses used in the performance of Mandiani are used to delineate a portion of an existent aesthetic.

This study indicates the presence of an aesthetic code for performing Mandiani encompassing a multiplicity of values. When participating in Mandiani, African-Americans bring complex sentiments in their desire to connect with Africa culturally: the conviction of their genetic birthright toAfrican culture, preferred patterns of visual and bodily cues, a particular sense of harmonic form in music, preferred gender roles in the social setting, and many other considerations. Aesthetic views which are realized from this involvement with Mandiani reflect: 1) an African-American position on Africa and African culture; 2) a social aesthetic of African-Americans; 3) physical elements in the African-American aesthetic; 4) interpersonal values in the African-American aesthetic; 5) individual aesthetic values; 6) conceptual practices or modes of operation; and 7) metaphysical beliefs. There are also basic theories in the African-American aesthetic which can be developed from this study. The following is a summary of these findings on aesthetics:

The African-American Position on Africa and African Culture

1. African-Americans would like to believe the material presented by continental African and American national, regional, and local performing companies is a true and accurate depiction of that activity as it takes place on the African continent, even though the degree of authenticity is not always known.

2. There is usually a strong commitment given byAfrican-American participants to representing the art form as accurately as their information, financial resources and beliefs will allow.

3. African-Americans can and do fulfill their desire to dress themselves in clothing that represents Africa. The interpretation can be in a contemporary western design or in conservative African colors and design concepts.

4. Financial resources and discretionary dollars are usually not available in the Black community to support local and touring companies. The community is more willing to support culture presenters. Their support for Africa is shown through political commentary when publicly voiced.

5. African music and dance is considered an art form in the United States by African-Americans.

6. African related movement and music styles are generally present in African-American youth culture. The fact that they exist reinforces aesthetic values placed in the movement style present in Mandiani.

7. The performer would prefer to present in a visual setting which clearly represents the African context.

8. A sentimental notion exists that the best items to own for aesthetic and historic reference are made from traditional African materials.

9. Participants believe that music and dance movements carry socio-cultural messages communicated in African society. Individuals look for assistance in interpreting music and dance, whether it is directly translatable or only understood as metaphor.

10. Personal gratification is derived from physical connection to indigenous African culture.

11. Volume along with rhythmic complexity are components credited for creating excitement and attracting individuals to African music. The decibel level capable on the djimbe and the diun diun have proven to be a primary attraction in Mande music.

12. African-Americans believe that certain behavioral characteristics exhibited in the United States by African-Americans are genetically encoded and natural. In performing these behaviors, they reinforce the connection to their ancestry.

13. The individuals involved in the practice of African music and dance believe it is their responsibility to preserve their cultural link with Africa.

Social Aesthetics of African-Americans

1. A communal activity is preferred above an individualistic or solo activity.

2. Characteristics found in the movement and music styles of Mandiani and other African dances are attractive to

African-Americans. The social grouping in the community of performers is based on this common attraction.

3. For many individuals, the commitment to African culture is realized as both a cultural and recreational endeavor.

4. It is important that songs are represented in any presentation of African music if possible.

5. In singing, there is a strong tendency among African-Americans to harmonize the melodies.

6. Educating people about Africa and keeping an African presence in the African-American community are the primary goals in presenting the music and dance of Africa to the community at large.

7. The class and the ensemble are places for social interaction. They also provide an environment in which male/female interaction as well as gender specific group activity can occur.

8. The music and dance arena provides an acceptable atmosphere for social procedures which are closer to traditional African practices than western concepts. At the same time, this platform can support contemporary views held by some community members about sexual equality through business management and the ideas about drumming as a purely masculine activity.

9. Female dancers are openly congratulatory to other dancers in the class and rehearsal setting.

10. The male dancer is much less likely to offer words of encouragement to other male dancers. There may be a silent visual acknowledgment but rarely overt congratulations. There is also a strong competitive spirit in male dance performance.

11. Male drummers are less inhibited in offering comments and suggestions on performance. Female drummers generally follow this male drummer pattern.

12. Most ensembles, groups and classes meet in the African-American community through a sense of responsibility to the community, regardless of where the participants may live.

13. Participation in performing ensembles is based primarily on ethnicity, a concept supported by the African-American community.

14. Physical location, social and interpersonal concerns often deter the participation of those not associated with the African-American community.

15. The performance of African music and dance is more aesthetically pleasing if it is performed by those with obvious genetic/racial links to African culture. Groups and classes which have a large percentage of African-American participants attract other African-Americans.

16. Possibly the most attractive aspect of the dance class or ensemble gathering is the unity of purpose, shared objectives to learn and participate in a commonly agreed upon activity which is based on the premise and content of African music and dance.

17. A mixed gender affiliation is preferred over single gender gatherings.

18. The desire is to keep access to music and dance activity within and for the general African-American community, rather than an exclusive or closed circle of participants.

19. In the African-American community, oral tradition is a primary means for information dissemination.

20. Geographic separation experienced by performing groups existing in major metropolitan areas across the country, local language or colloquial terminology, customs and practices, as well as masters of the craft residing in their respective regions continue to define the presentation of Mandiani and other African music and dance in the United States.

21. A competitive spirit is displayed in both drumming and dancing, yet a communal sense is retained.

Physical Elements in the African-American Aesthetic

1. Expectations in the singing style of the African-American while singing African songs is that the singers will use a clear, unaffected voice. The range of possible vocal techniques exhibited in other African-American vocal styles is generally not exploited.

2. The harmonic interpretation of African song by African-Americans includes tonic, sub-dominant, and dominant chord functions as experienced in western harmonic

structure. These sounds are reminiscent of harmonic practices found in the Black church.

3. The instrument responsible for the lowest frequencies should have a very clearly stated primary pulse with a distinct rhythmic orientation. The example played by African-Americans in Mandiani is the single diun diun part. Melodic contour is not required in the Mandiani diun diun part.

4. In the upper drum frequencies, sharp polyrhythmic accents are essential as exhibited in the rhythms played on the djimbe for Mandiani.

5. Volume along with rhythmic complexity create excitement. The diun diun and the djimbe are a primary attraction in Mande music because of these sonic capabilities.

6. Auxiliary percussion instruments such as the shekere, rattles, and cowbell are often played by individuals who are not designated drummers and are used to augment impromptu drumming sessions.

7. Sound enhancers such as kesingkesings and small bells are recognized as an important component of the total ensemble sound, and seasoned players use these devices more frequently than others outside of the performance setting. Drummers who do not regularly use sound enhancers often prefer the pure drum tone.

8. The sensual quality in Mandiani is most often related to the performer's physique, musculature, other anatomical features, or certain gestures and movements chosen for solo display. Dance movements which emphasize the torso and pelvis may be introduced by certain solo performers. These movements are not part of the general movement vocabulary normally seen and presented by African-American ensembles for Mandiani.

9. The idea that Mandiani has physically demanding requirements subsequently deters individuals who might otherwise participate.

10. In the 1990s, part of the concept of physical beauty in the United States is that individuals must present a slim and lean appearance conforming to western ideas. Strict adherence to this concept is not a primary concern to the Mandiani

population in the United States. Less than fifty percent of the American participants were concerned with this issue. In Sénégal, the wish is for girls and boys as they mature to gain weight.

11. There are anatomical characteristics in Black physiology that are in opposition to the western aesthetic such as kinky hair, full lips, and fully proportioned hips and buttocks. These characteristics are focal points in the African and African-American aesthetic.

Interpersonal Values in the African-American Aesthetic

1. The class and the performing ensemble are places for social interaction.

2. Learning in the African-American community relies principally on aural and visual perceptions and is often achieved through intuitive learning. Continuity between these two approaches can be aided or enhanced with contemporary technology.

3. The aural tradition relies on verbal verification of procedure and process.

4. Males are unlikely to offer words of encouragement to other males. Females are generally more encouraging in nature than males.

5. Traditional female roles and strengths that were gender specific for effecting changes or exerting control in a subtle fashion have been augmented for women by the social revolution in the United States. The possibility for women to make open and direct contributions to African-American society is opening.

6. The competitive spirit is realized in the approach taken by dancers in their efforts to reproduce individually distinct movements. The same observation can be made of many drummers. Mandiani drum music can provide musically distinct and significant parts which complement the sound matrix.

7. Sensuous or sexy movements are chosen by gregarious performers to be used as solo dance steps.

8. Comfort is derived from the concept of independence through achieving recognition as a soloist, as well as the

interdependence found in performing both the music and the dance.

9. Within the ensemble, there is a close sense of community.

Conceptual Practices or Aesthetic Modes of Operation

1. The possibility exists for African-American identity traits to be included in Mandiani resulting from the processes of adaptation and transformation.

2. The intuitive process is the natural procedure within the African-American community for learning music and dance. It is accomplished by assimilating visual, auditory, and kinetic information. A language has been developed to accompany instruction. This is done to provide aural systems for communicating rhythms and movements. An example is the use of vocables by drummers.

3. In an environment which does not exclude the element of play, Mandiani permits and encourages a degree of individual creativity.

4. Minor variations in performance are accepted because these deviations are secondary to an exciting class or performance.

5. Stability in class and performance results from knowing what to expect, or being familiar with the range of variables from which fellow performers draw their performance materials. These variables define performance boundaries.

6. The ideal for many African-Americans is to have African articles decorated with traditional African themes.

7. Drummers desire quick access to a performance-ready instrument without loss of time in preparation.

8. The time involved in assembly is justification for not routinely using sound enhancing devices.

9. Musical instruments will take on a rhythmic rather than a melodic function, even if they are constructed to produce melody.

10. African definitions for sensuous movement or behavior are not usually available or employed in determining which dance steps will be used by African-American dancers.

11. The African-American concept of sensuality is employed when evaluating certain performers and it is occasionally the motivating dynamic when a dancer chooses a solo dance step.
12. Erect posture is one of the western characteristics found in the African-American approach to African dance.
13. The youth culture in both Afro- and Euro-American society has assimilated dynamic African characteristics into contemporary popular dance often without recognizing the association.
14. The concept of "pose" is used when performing African dance in the United States, and it serves to identify the way in which African dance is perceived by the student and performer.
15. African music and dance is regularly conceived as a staged activity in the United States.
16. Volume and intense activity is viewed as therapy by the participants in a variety of situations.

Individual or Personal Aesthetic Values

1. The ensemble can support traditional, contemporary, and personal concepts of equality of the sexes.
2. Social factors in the community environment can be deterrents to individual musicians and dancers.
3. The performance of African music and dance is a birthright, and it is to be respected as such.
4. Participants are attracted to the physical nature of the Mande style on a very personal level.
5. The assembly time required is justification for not using additional sound devices for every drumming occasion.
6. The desire to hear pure tone can be the motivation for not using sound devices such as kesingkesings all the time.
7. Involvement with African music and dance is internally motivated, not financially spurred.
8. A mixed gender setting is desired for the African drum and dance activity.
9. It is desired that African drum and dance activity itself is not dependent on technology. Recording technology can augment group meetings.
10. The expected behavior for African-American males is the internalization of any reaction that might be conceived

as physical and emotional weakness in performance and social settings. This behavior defines the image of the African-American male.

11. African-Americans in the performance of African music and dance use western cosmetic products including lipstick, rouge, and nail polish rather than traditional African substances, techniques, and concepts.

12. Scarification is not expected of African-American men or women in the portrayal of African culture; however, calluses, an occupationally caused example of scarification among drummers, is carried with a sense of pride.

13. Sensual or sexy movements are chosen by performers for personal rather than socio-cultural reasons.

14. Individuals involved in African music and dance might be classified as "Type A Personalities."

15. Elders in the African-American community do not participate in Mande style dances, even when there is a desire to do so, because of the perceived physical demands.

16. Pride is taken in Black physiology and has become a focal point in the African-American aesthetic.

17. Having one drum that fulfills all of one's sonic, visual, and physical criteria would be ideal for most drummers. The improbability of this condition is offered as the reason for owning multiple instruments.

18. For drummers, physical connectedness to the drum is a desirable characteristic of the Mande music culture.

19. Physical connectedness to the culture through visual display of one's person is a desirable characteristic for dancers and drummers.

20. It is important for participants to experience the power of self for emotional balance. To be the designated soloist for a brief period of time allows one to experience this phenomenon in addition to the ensemble mosaic.

The Metaphysical Aesthetic

1. The Mandiani community is likely to accept the existence of phenomena that are scientifically inexplicable. They are willing to support spiritual or mystical explanations offered in the presentation of African music and dance as part of the culture.
2. The belief that time is organic, rather than mechanical, is reflected in the idea that an individual is often manipulated by a higher power or events not within his or her control.
3. The Mandiani community believes in the powers of music and dance to affect physical and mental dispositions.

The above observations provide specific insights into the what, how, and why of African-American aesthetics and the larger Black aesthetic. The approach used here might also be helpful when examining Afro- and Euro-American culture or other multi-ethnic communities. The study of continuity and change affecting both Afro and Euro cultures in the United States might benefit from issues raised. The questions raised need not be ethnically structured. Each of the specific areas examined may be expanded and used in parallel examinations of other societies and cultures in the United States or beyond.

Conclusion

Mandiani music and dance exists in West Africa among the Mande cultures as both a folkloric presentation to the world and a vibrant representation of their cultural heritage still very much a part of their lives. This music and dance has been passed from generation to generation and through each one, the creativity of the Mande people has generated countless movement variations and solo drum patterns rooted in aesthetic perceptions which can be viewed as both specific to the Mande people, and in a general sense, relevant to people of the African diaspora.

It is important to offer descriptions of what Mandiani might have been in the distant past, what it is in the West African countries where it exists today, and its transformation in the distant culture of the African-American community. In this text Mandiani serves as a window through which we examine aspects of the African-American aesthetic and subsequently, views which are a part of the greater Black aesthetic.

The drum and dance ensemble which performs Mandiani can be seen as a metaphor of African-American thinking. A relationship to sound and sonic properties is exemplified in the rhythms played and performance techniques used on the djimbe. This drum reflects the sensitivity to frequency range and dynamic levels which are found in the African-American community and other Black communities around the world. The rhythmic textures, stratification, and independent nature of the drum parts also reflect individual and group thinking. The need for general conformity yet the desire for individual identity is seen in both the drum and dance activity.

The physical act of creating music and dance is a part of many cultures. The elements used in creating Mandiani represent qualities and positions found in the Black aesthetic. These realities in the Black aesthetic take music and dance beyond the concept of art. Mandiani is an example of how the physicality of drumming and dancing serves much more than the body. Music and dance in the Black aesthetic is not only entertainment but also functional. In the African-American community, Mandiani has provided a cultural/historical link to the African continent. For many participants, this is a physical activity which takes place in a social environment with a well defined male/female relationship desired by many. The role designations of dancers and drummers allow the individual to have control over immediate circumstance.

The aesthetic values represented here by no means represent the sum total of aesthetic values held by the African-American community; nonetheless, they do provide insights into aesthetic thinking and how these aesthetic values manifest themselves through Mandiani. Nketia said aesthetic concerns in the performing arts should not be limited to that which is deemed beautiful to see, touch, and hear.[4] In the responses given by music and dance presenters, and the audiences for Mandiani, "beautiful" was the term used to express a sensuous response to this activity involving sound, color, clothing styles, and the physical appearance of the performers. There were also intuitive cognitions involved in the presentation and reception of Mandiani which permeate the African-American culture. These cognitions include rhythm, frequency orientation, and energy levels in both sound and movement style, all of which are physical manifestations of aesthetic thought. Within the realm of the psyche, those less tangible areas of emotion, personality, and metaphysical awareness provide a foundation for aesthetic thinking. The way we think as a community is arrived at by community consensus. There is an intellectual side to forming this consensus, but more often we perceive it as an emotional one. Mande culture has an emotional appeal to many people of the world but it has proven to be a significant representation of new world Africans in the United States.

List of Informants

ANGELA DUNREATH ADDISON began her professional training in dance in St. Louis with Ludmila Dukoudovsky. Her African dance training took place at the American Dance Festival where she trained and performed with Chuck Davis. Miss Addison earned her B.F.A. in dance performance and choreography at Arizona State University and she currently holds an elementary certification from the Labanotation Bureau in New York City.

All of the dance notation used for this study was prepared by Miss Addison from in-person demonstrations, video taped examples and personal discussions. This material was paid for through a grant provided by the University Committee on African and African-American Studies at Arizona State University. The transcriptions were compiled over a five month period from May to September 1992.

ABDUL AZIZ AHMED is an African-American from Bronx, New York, where he studied with master drummer Ladji Camara. Ahmed has taught classes in drumming and dance around the country and performed with several professional dance companies in the United States. He currently lives in Tucson, Arizona where he has his own performing group, Nonfoulé.

KARIAMU WELSH ASANTE is a dance historian and ethnographer working in African and African-American dance. She has lectured and performed throughout the country. From 1981 to 1983 she was a Fulbright professor at the University of Zimbabwe. During that period, Dr. Asante also served as director and resident choreographer for the National Dance Company of Zimbabwe. Since 1982, Dr. Asante has presented workshops and lectures on the *Mfundala* dance technique which she developed to teach fundamentals of African dance. She has several publications on African and African-American art and aesthetics to her credit.

MALANG BAYO is Sénégalese. He danced with the National Ballet of Sénégal for five years from 1984 to 1989 until he came to the United States in 1989. Since then, he has taught classes around the country. Bayo lived in New York City for two years and is currently living in Southern California where he performs with several African dance companies including his own, the Sona Sane West African Dance Ensemble. Mr. Bayo made the arrangements for a three week stay in Sénégal for members of the Kawambé Drum and Dance Ensemble during the summer of 1992.

BASORY IBRAHIMA BANGOURA is of the Susu people of Guinea. He has performed as a dancer with the national dance companies of Guinea and Sénégal. He has also served a choreographer and costumer for professional dance companies in Sénégal and the United States.

M'BEMBA BANGOURA is of the Susu people of Guinea. He has played the Djimbe with the National Ballet of Guinea for fifteen years.

CHIEF BEY is one of the pioneers in African drumming in the United States. He has performed with and for other pioneers in African dance including Pearl Primus and accompanied her on one of her early trips to Africa.

MELVIN DEAL is director of the African Heritage Theater in Washington, D.C. He is a product of the Olatunji school in New York. He has visited and studied in several West African countries. The African Heritage Theater provides classes in African drumming and dance. During my visit there during the summer of 1990, the students, all part of a summer youth program, performed dances of the Mande cultures, including Mandiani.

ABUBAKR DIARRA is an African-American living in New York. He began his studies in African dance in New York and subsequently had an opportunity to study in Africa with dancers in the National Ballets of Guinea and Sénégal. Diarra currently teaches African dance in New York City.

OUMOUKALTOM DIOP was a dance instructor during a four week visit to Dakar, Sénégal during the summer of 1989, arranged by Mor Thiam. She has danced with international touring companies assembled by Mor Thiam and with the National Ballet of Sénégal.

KEBA DIOUF was interviewed in the summer of 1989 during a four week research trip to Sénégal. At that time, he was the costume designer for the National Ballet Company of Sénégal.

C.K. GANYO is a drummer and dancer from Ghana. For many years he collected music and dance from the various parts of that country for the National Arts Council of Ghana. Mr. Ganyo has lived in the United States for more than seven years, teaching the music, dance and folklore of Ghana. He currently teaches at Arizona State University.

MEDOUNE YACINE GUEYE was the djimbe drummer and teacher in Dakar during a four week visit to Sénégal in the summer of 1989. He was born into a family of drummers, plays a variety of drums and has performed with the National Ballet of Sénégal.

PATDRO HARRIS is an African-American dancer formerly of New York City now living in Atlanta. He has studied modern dance and African dance, as well as other western forms. He currently performs and teaches in Atlanta.

TREVOR HALL is a professor and African historian at Arizona State University specializing in pre-colonial Africa.

AIEDOO HOLMES is a djimbe drummer living in Washington, D.C. He operates a small West African import business, and has his own performing group. He frequently travels to West Africa to study the kora, the balafon, and the dances of Guinea.

ASSANE KONTE is a dancer born in the Casamance region of Sénégal. He has travelled and performed extensively among the Mande cultures of West Africa. In the United States, he performed with Mor Thiam and Melvin Deal, and formed the Konkourian West African Dance Company.

ABDOU KOUNTA was born in Mauritania and raised in Dakar, Sénégal. He came to the United States to drum with Assane Konte. Abdou has taught and performed in the Washington, D.C. area for almost fifteen years.

BABATUNDE OLATUNJI, born in Nigeria, moved to the United States in 1950 and graduated from Morehouse College in 1954. He then moved to New York City to attend graduate school at New York University. He went on to perform widely and to make many significant recordings such as *Drums of Passion,* first released in 1959.

SANGA OF THE VALLEY is an African-American from the Caribbean who has performed with Babatunde Olatunji for more than seven years. As part of various drumming communities in New York he has performed in a wide variety of settings.

JALAL SHARRIFF is an African-American who has studied African percussion with well-known African percussionists in and around New York City since 1968. His teachers include Ladji Camara, Famadou Camara, Souleymane Diop, Ibrahim Camara, and Abdou Kounta. He has been a featured artist with many performing ensembles, and he has served as musical director for the Chuck Davis Dance Company.

NAFISA SHARRIFF is an African-American who has studied, performed and taught African-American dance in New York City for almost twenty years. Her African dance teachers were Youseff Koumbassa, Ibrahim Camara, Souleymane Diop, Assane Konte, Chuck Davis and Hazel Bryant. She has choreographed African dances for many groups.

BRADLEY SIMMONS is an African-American ethnic percussionist from New York City. He has played trap set, conga drums and djimbe. He directs a group of hand drummers that perform music of Africa and the diaspora.

MOR THIAM, former djimbe drummer with the National Ballet of Sénégal, now lives in the United States. He has directed his own company, performed with many other groups, he has brought performing companies from Sénégal to tour the United States, and he has taught djimbe playing in the United States for almost twenty years. Mor's wife, KINE THIAM, has danced and taught Sénégalese dance in the United States with her husband.

OMAR THIAM is a performing artist of national stature in Sénégal. He is the resident artist at the Cultural Center in Kaolack, Sénégal, and directs his own performing ensemble which has toured internationally representing Sénégal.

Notes

Chapter One

1. Irwin Edman 1967, 21.
2. *ibid.*, 28.
3. *ibid.*, 24,
4. *The Anthropology of Music* , p. 260.
5. *Psychical Distance as a Factor in Art and an Aesthetic Principle*, (Bullough 1912); cited by Alan P. Merriam, *The Anthropology of Music*, (Evanston: Northwestern Univ. Press), p. 261.
6. *History and Appreciation of Art*, (Longman 1949, 14) cited by Alan P. Merriam, *The Anthropology of Music*, (Evanston: Northwestern Univ. Press), p. 263.
7. *Aesthetic Judgment and Relativism*, Crowley 1958, cited by Alan P. Merriam, *The Anthropology of Music*, (Evanston: Northwestern Univ. Press), p. 268.
8. This term resulted from dialogue between Caribbean and West African students during the 1930s in centers like Paris. Negritude, so labelled by Césaire, reflected the growing awareness of black consciousness (Magaga Alot 1973, 71). "Negritude as an assertion of black aesthetics could be expressed as a defeatist and apologetic black attitude or a taken-for-granted revolutionary and proud attitude" (Zirimu 1973, 69).
9. Molefi Kete Asante, "Afrocentricity and Culture," in *African Culture: The Rhythms of Unity*. Edited by Molefi Kete Asante and Kariamu Welsh Asante. Trenton: African World Press, Inc., 1990, 6.
10. An interview with Melvin Deal in 1990.
11. A variety of spellings have been encountered for this drum. I have elected to use *djimbe* which is the spelling used in the promotional materials provided by the Guinea National Ballet Company.

Chapter Two

1. This spelling will be used and is the Malinke name for the instrument according to notes prepared by the National Dance Company of Guinea. In the same source, Sambanyi is identified as the name used for this instrument by the Soso ethnic group of Guinea.
2. Mondet and Drame 1979. The name as spoken by the people is actually Bamana.
3. Precolonial Black Africa, 1987, 119.
4. Bernard Mondet and Adama Drame 1979.
5. Mondet and Drame 1979.
6. *Figure 4* only represents one half of the complete movement cycle. The second half of the step cycle is always executed in the opposite direction.
7. The dotted quarter note would equal 120 pulses per minute.
8. The dotted quarter note equals 160 pulses per minute.

9. Raffia is a natural fiber either created from palm fibers or long blades of dried grass. This fiber is used to make articles of clothing which resemble a grass skirt. However, the garment is never referred to in these terms. It is simply called raffia.

10. The vibrating pattern on of the djimbe drumhead is similar to the vibrating pattern found on the timpani. The entire drumhead moves together to produce the bass or fundamental tone. There are also a series of smaller vibrating points on the drumhead which which form rings or nodes moving from the center to the edge of the drum. By striking the drumhead at certain points away from the center of the drum the solo "slap" sound (just the highest overtones) can be set in motion.

11. For additional descriptions of the basic drum sounds and their variations see *Drum Talk*, Mor Thiam 1980, 8-13.

12. I was told there was one drummer missing that night. That may account for the absence of the principal part heard in every other example of Mandiani noted.

13. Mondet and Drame 1979.

14. Webster 1973, 257.

15. In ancient societies of Africa, when the cowrie was used as a form of money, the cowrie covered bra would have been considered part of the bride's dowry (Asante 1990).

Chapter Three

1. See *Ethnomusicology* 3: 1976, 529-530 for Harwood's original discussion.

2. "Melanins are biological polymers responsible for pigmentation in humans and animals. Melanin-containing cells are present in the inner ear. The content of melanosomes in the inner ear melanocytes varies from race to race and from one individual to another in accordance with skin pigmentation (Barrenas and Lindgren 1990, 97).

3. Although the general frequency range for drums is very wide, usually there is a perceived pitch. For the solo sound on the djimbe, this perceived pitch falls between B5 and D6 (987.7666 and 1174.6591 Hz).

4. The tone resonates between E4 and B4 (329.6275 and 493.8833 Hz).

5. The diun diun in the United States is preferred to resonate between D2 and E2 (73.4161 and 82.4068 Hz). The drums heard on the compact disk of Les Ballet Africains from Guinea has the doundoun pitched between G2 and A2 (97.9988 and 109.9999 Hz), the sangbé near B2 and C3 (123.4708 and 130.8127 Hz), and the kenkeni at A3 (219.9999 Hz).

6. Conversation with Assane Konti in 1990. Rouget discusses the existent theories surrounding drumming, low frequencies, high dynamic levels, and their connection to altered consciousness, or ecstasy in his book *Music and Trance* (1985).

7. There is one notable exception to the melody concept in Sénégal during the celebration known as Gamu Kahone. At this celebration, there is music which is played solely by seven diun diuns.

8. There are examples of melodic process in Ghanaian drumming which are discussed by Nketia in *Drumming in Akan Societies* (1963), Locke in *Drum Gahu* (1987), and Anku in *Procedures in African Drumming* (1988).

9. These sounds are part of the "Classification of Consonants According to Principal Physiological Features of Articulation" (Curtis 1978, 46-47).

10. Krumhansl 1991, 292.

11. *Ashé* is translated from the Yoruba language in Nigeria to mean "so be it." In the class context, this gesture is intended to mean "thank you."

12. Kwabena Nketia, *The Music of Africa* (1974, 57).

13. Francis Bebey, *African Music, A Peoples Art*, 1975, 102.

14. Kwabena Nketia, *The Music of Africa* (1974, 57).

15. Kwabena Nketia, *The Music of Africa* (1974, 100).

16. According to Asante, the Mfundalai Technique is one of two African dance techniques used in modern dance companies (Asante, 1985, 402).

17. Average community people may be just as adept in music and dance and remain outside of the professional realm.

18. In observing classes and performances by African dancers, these intricacies and finite movements occur as a result of large gestures and are very often representative of an individual's performing style rather than a specified directive. It must be understood that many of these stylistic gestures can be idiomatic as well as idiosyncratic.

19. The stratification of the Mandiani rhythm in this study will begin with four beats per cycle (measure), equal in length at the lowest stratum. The first level divides each pulse into two equal parts, the second divides each pulse into three equal parts and the third into four. Rhythmically, these ideas are prevalent among drummers. William Oscar Anku discusses this issue in *Procedures in African Drumming: A Study of Akan/Ewe Traditions and African Drumming in Pittsburgh*. Ann Arbor, Mich.: University Microfilms, 1989.

20. Welsh Asante 1990. Asante illustrated a bounce initiated from the knees and reflected in the whole torso.

21. In an effort to understand the focus on hand and forearm exercises, I referred to an exercise manual by Judy Alter: "The ligaments that hold all the bones in your wrists and hands together are, in many cases, looser than other in your body because the looseness allows your hands the mobility they need. . . . Your hands have many muscles to allow you to move your bones around in [a] variety of directions. Your arm muscles provide your wrist their mobility. So do your finger muscles. The muscles in your palm move your wrists and your fingers. Some of your finger muscles start on your forearms and some of them start in your palm (Alter 1986; 75).

22. There are examples in available percussion performance and ethnomusicological literature. David Locke introduced a collection of vocal

sounds derived from his studies of Ewe drumming in his publication, *Drum Gahu* (1987, 40). The rhythms associated with this dance of the Anlo/Ewe people can serve as an illustration. Mor Thiam (1980) prepared the booklet *Drum Talk*, which offers the vocables used by djimbe drummers in Sénégal.

23. Dane Archer, *How to Expand Your Social Intelligence Quotient, S.I.Q.* New York: M. Evans and Company, Inc., 1980.

24. Witsen 1981, XV..

25. Bebey 1984, 92.

26. Huet 1978, 28.

27. Alan Lomax, *Folk Song Style and Culture*. New Brunswick: Transaction, Inc. 1978, 256-258).

28. Chuck Davis, *Dancing Through West Africa*. Davis explains the arm motion seen in the dance Lingin (or Lingingo) mimics the flapping of bird wings. Another interpretation was offered by Mor Thiam during a dance lecture given in Casamance in August of 1989. He said, "The movements mean if I hit you please forgive me because I am so involved with the dance, I might not be able to control my hands, so forgive me." This might be more easily interpreted as a social courtesy than an explanation of the dance movement.

29. For a detailed discussion and list of these fetishes see William S. Simmons, Eyes of the Night, *Witchcraft Among a Sénégalese People*. Boston: Little Brown and Company, Inc. 1971.

30. A Sénégalese woman, Madjigen Seck, explained that if the henna mixture is left for a few hours the resultant pattern is red. If however it remains overnight, the pattern will be black and lasts for three or more months.

31. Conversation with Madjigen Seck.

32. Trevor Hall 1991.

33. Ahmed, 1990.

34. Among the practicing Yoruba in the United States or those musicians and dancers who are familiar with Yoruba culture, the Igunnu-ko may be the primary image portrayed as a cylinder made of fabric which grows very tall with the dancer inside. This figure often begins dancing no more than two or three feet tall. The skill of the individual dancing inside the fabric tube is displayed as the Igunnu-ko grows to more than eight or ten feet tall during the course of the dance. By the end of the dance, the figure has returned to the original height or lower. This particular mask is probably the most familiar in the African-American community.

Chapter Four

1. Dorothy L. Pennington, "Time in African Culture," in *African Culture: The Rhythms of Unity*, 1990, 123-140.

2. *ibid.*, 136.

3. *ibid.*, 137.

4. "The Aesthetic Dimensions in Ethnomusicological Studies," *World of Music* 26, 1: 3-28. 1984, 14.

Bibliography

Agawu, V. Kofi. "The Impact of Language on Musical Composition in Ghana: An Introduction to the Musical Style of Ephraim Amu," *Ethnomusicology* 28,1 (1984): 37-73.

Alot, Magaga. Negritude, "Black Aesthetics—The Myths and Realities of the Black Fact," in *Black Aesthetics: Papers from a Colloquium* Held at the University of Nairobi, June, 1971. Edited by Pio Zirimu and Andrew Gurr. Nairobi: East African Literature Bureau, 1973.

Alter, Judy. *Stretch and Strengthen*. Boston: Houghton Mifflin Company, 1986 .

Anku, William Oscar. *Procedures in African Drumming: A Study of Akan/Ewe Traditions and African Drumming in Pittsburgh*. Ann Arbor, MI: University Microfilms, 1989.

Apel, Willi. *Harvard Dictionary of Music*. Cambridge: Belknap Press of Harvard University Press, 1969.

Archer, Dane. *How to Expand Your Social Intelligence Quotient, S.I.Q.* New York: M. Evans and Company, Inc., 1980.

Asante, Molefi K. "Afrocentricity and Culture," in *African Culture: The Rhythms of Unity*. Edited by Molefe Kete Asante and Kariamu Welsh Asante. Trenton: African World Press, Inc., 1990.

Bailey, Covert. *The New Fit or Fat*. Boston: Houghton Mifflin Company, 1991.

Barrenas, Marie-Louise, and Fedrik Lindgren. "The Influence of Inner Ear Melanin on Susceptibility to TTS In Humans," *Scandinavian Audiology* 19, 2 (1990): 97-102.

Bebey, Francis. *African Music: A People's Art*. Westport: Lawrence Hill & Co., Publishers, Inc., 1975.

Begho, F. *Black Dance Continuum: Reflections on the Heritage Connection Between African Dance and Afro-American Jazz Dance*. 2 Vols. Ann Arbor, MI: University Microfilms, 1985.

Blacking, John. "Field Work in African Music," in *Reflections on Afro-American Music*, Translated by Dominique Rene de Lerma. Kent: Kent State University Press (1973), 207-221.

Boateng, Felix. "African Tradition Education: A Tool for Intergenerational Communication," in *African Culture: The Rhythms of Unity*. Edited by Molefe Kete Asante and Kariamu Welsh Asante. Trenton: Africa World Press, Inc. (1990), 109-122.

Bohannan, Paul, and Philip Curtin. *Africa and Africans*. Prospect Heights: Waveland Press, Inc., 1988.

Boykin, A. Wade and Brenda A. Allen. "Rhythmic-Movement Facilitation of Learning in Working-Class Afro-American Children," *Journal of Genetic Psychology*, 149, 3 (1988): 355-348.

Burnim, Mellonee V. "The Black Gospel Music Tradition: A Complex of Ideology, Aesthetic, and Behavior," in *More Than Dancing—Essays on Afro-American Music and Musicians*. Edited by Irene V. Jackson. Westport: Greenwood Press (1985), 147-168.

Cable, George W. "The Dance in Place Congo," *Century Magazine* 31 (February 1886): 517-532.

Calder, Angus. "An Open Letter to Pio Zirimu," in *Black Aesthetics: Papers from a Colloquium Held at the University of Nairobi, June, 1971*. Edited by Pio Zirimu and Andrew Gurr. Nairobi: East African Literature Bureau, 1973.

Chernoff, John Miller. *African Rhythm and African Sensibility*. Chicago: University of Chicago Press, 1979.

Coolen, Michael T. "The Wolof Xalam Tradition of the Sénégambia," *Ethnomusicology* 27, 3 (1983): 447-499.

Curtin, Philip D. *The Atlantic Slave Trade, A Census*. Madison: University of Wisconsin Press, 1969.

Curtis, James F., ed. *Processes and Disorders of Human Communication*. Harper & Row Publishers, 1978.

Cushman, Anne. "Drumming to The Rhythms of Life," *Yoga Journal*, January/February (1993), 44.

DuBois, William E. Burghardt. "Of the Sorrow Songs," in *The Black Aesthetic*. edited by Addison Gale 1971, Garden City: Doubleday and Company, Inc., 1971.

Darden, Ellington. *New High Intensity Bodybuilding*. New York: Putnam Publishing Co., 1990.

Davis, Nathan. *Writings in Jazz*. 3rd ed. Scottsdale, AZ: Gorsuch Scarisbrick Publishers 1985.

de Lerme, Dominique-René. *Reflections on Afro-American Music*. Kent: The Kent State University Press, 1973.

Diallo, Yaya and Mitchell Hall. *The Healing Drum: African Wisdom Teachings*. Rochester, Vermont: Destiny Books, 1989.

Dietz, Betty Warner, and Michael Babatundi Olatunji. *Musical Instruments of Africa*. New York: John Day Company, 1965.

Dorsey, David. "Prolegomena for Black Aesthetics," in *Black Aesthetics: Papers from a Colloquium held at the University of Nairobi, June, 1971*. Edited by Pio Zirimu and Andrew Gurr. Nairobi: East African Literature Bureau, 1973.

Drame, Adama. Rhythms of the Manding—Adama Drame (Jembe) Unesco Collection, Musical Sources, *The Language of Rhythm III-3*. (liner notes) London: Philips 6586 042 (LP disc), 1979.

Edman, Irwin. *Arts And The Man*. New York: W.W. Norton, 1967.

Emery, Lynne Fauley. *Black Dance in the United States from 1619 to 1970*. Palo Alto, Calif.: National Press Books, 1972.

Epstein, Dena J. *Sinful Tunes and Spirituals*. Chicago: University of Chicago Press, 1977.

Fierce, Milfred C. *African-American Interest in Africa and Interaction with West Africa: The Origins of the Pan-African Idea in the United States 1900-1919*. New York: Columbia University Microfilm, 1976.

Friedman, Robert Alan. *Making an Abstract World Concrete: Knowledge Competence and Structural Dimensions of Performance Among Bata Drummers in Santaria*. Ann Arbor, MI: University Microfilms, 1982.

Galeota, Jr., Joseph A. "Kinka," *Percussive Notes* 23, 4 (1985): 55-57.

Gardner, Howard. *Unschooled Mind: How Children Think and How Schools Should Teach*. New York: Basic Books, 1991.

Glaze, Anita J. *Art and Death in a Senufo Village*. Bloomington: Indiana University Press, 1981.

Glover, Jean Ruth. Pearl Primus: *Cross-Cultural Pioneer of American Dance*. Ann Arbor, MI: University Microfilms, 1990.

Goffin, Robert. *JAZZ: From the Congo to the Metropolitan*. New York: Da Capo Press, 1975.

Goines, Margaretta Bobo. "African Retentions in the Dance of the Americas," *Cord Dance Research Annual* 5 (1973): 207-229.

Hanna, Judith Lynne. "African Dance as Education," *Impulse — Annual of Contemporary Dance* (1965): 48-56.

_____. "Africa's New Traditional Dance," *Ethnomusicology*, 9, 1 (1965): 13-21.

_____. "Field Research in African Dance: Opportunities and Utilities," *Ethnomusicology* 12, 1 (1968): 101-106.

_____. "African Dance Frame by Frame," *Journal of Black Studies* 19, 4 (1989): 422-441.

Harrison, Frank L., Mantle Hood, and Claude V. Palisca. *Musicology*. Englewood Cliffs: Prentice Hall, 1963.

Hart, Mickey. *Drumming at the Edge of Magic*. New York: Harper Collins Publishers, 1990.

Harwood, Dane L. "Universals in Music: A Perspective from Cognitive Psychology," *Ethnomusicology* 20, 3 (1976): 521-533.

Hood, Mantle. "The Reliability of Oral Tradition," *Journal of the American Musicological Society*, 12, 2-3 (1959): 201-209.

_____. *The Ethnomusicologist*. Kent: Kent State University Press, 1982.

Howard, George, "Culture Tales, A Narrative Approach to Thinking, Cross-Cultural Psychology, and Psychotherapy," *American Psychology* 46, 3 (1991): 187-197.

Huet, Michel. *The Dance, Art and Ritual of Africa*. New York: Random House, 1978

Hutchinson, Ann. *Labanotation: The System of Analyzing and Recording Movements*. 3rd, ed. New York: Theatre Arts Books, 1954.

Institute Géographique National. *Guinée*. Edition I, Paris, IGN., 1980.

Irvine, Judith T., and J. David Sapir. "Musical Style and Social Change Among the Kujamaat Diola," *Ethnomusicology* 20,1 (1976): 67-86.

Itoh, Setsu. *Consciousness and Unity Through Children's Dance Theatre: Redefinition of Traditional African Culture*. M.A. Thesis, City University of New York, 1990.

Jackson, Irene V., ed. *More Than Dancing—Essays on Afro-American Music and Musicians*. Westport: Greenwood Press, 1985.

Jackson, Marie Joyce. *The Performing Black Sacred Quartet: An Expression of Cultural Values and Aesthetics*. Bloomington: Indiana University Microfilm, 1988.

Johnson, J. H., ed. "Pearl Primus," *Ebony*, January (1951), 54-58.

Joiner, Betty. *Costumes for the Dance*. New York: A. A. Barnes & Company, 1937.

Kauffman, Robert. "African Rhythm: A Reassessment," *Ethnomusicology* 24, 3 (1980): 393-415.

Kealiinohomoku, Joann W. "Dance Culture as a Microcosm of Holistic Culture," *Cord Dance Research Annual* 6: (1974): 99-106.

_____."A Comparative Study of Dance as a Constellation of Motor Behaviors Among African and United States Negroes," *Cord Dance Research Annual* 7: (1976): 15-170.

Kinney, Sylvia. "Drummers in Dagbon: The Role of the Drummer in the Damba Festival," *Ethnomusicology* 14, 2 (1970): 258-265.

Knight, Roderic. *Mandinka Jaliya: Professional Music of the Gambia*. 2 Vols. Ann Arbor, MI: University Microfilms, 1973.

_____."The Style of Mandinka Music: A Study of Extracting Theory from Practice," *Selected Reports in Ethnomusicology, Studies in African Music* 5 (1984): 3-66.

Krumhansl, Carol L. "Music Psychology: Tonal Structures in Perception and Memory," *Annual Review of Psychology* 42 (1991): 277-303.

Langner, Lawrence. *The Importance of Wearing Clothes*. New York: Hastings House Publishers, 1959.

Les Ballets Africains: African Ballet of the Republic of Guinea, London, England: Doun Doumba DDB 40001 (Compact disc), 1991.

Locke, David. "Principles of Offbeat Timing and Cross-Rhythm in Southern Ewe Dance Drumming," *Ethnomusicology* 26, 2 (1982): 217-246.

_____. "The Rhythm of Takai," *Percussive Notes* 23, 4 (1985): 51-54.

_____. *Drum Gahu: The Rhythms of West African Drumming*. Tempe, AZ: White Cliffs Media, Inc., 1987.

Lomax, Alan. *Folk Song Style and Culture*. New Brunswick, New Jersey: Transaction, Inc., 1978.

Lugira, Aloysius M. "Black Aesthetics," in *Black Aesthetics: Papers from a Colloquium Held at the University of Nairobi, June, 1971*. Edited by Pio Zirimu and Andrew Gurr. Nairobi: East African Literature Bureau, 1973.

Maultsby, Portia K. "Africanisms in African-American Music," in *Africanisms In American Culture*, Edited by Joseph E. Holloway. Vol. 21. Bloomington: Indiana University Press (1990): 185-210.

_____. "West African Influences and Retentions in U.S. Black Music: A Sociocultural Study," in *More Than Dancing—Essays on Afro-American Music and Musicians*. Edited by Irene V. Jackson. Westport: Greenwood Press (1985), 25-57.

Mazrui, Ali. "Aesthetic Dualism and Creative Literature in East Africa," in *Black Aesthetics: Papers from a Colloquium Held at the University of Nairobi, June, 1971*. Edited by Pio Zirimu and Andrew Gurr. Nairobi: East African Literature Bureau, 1973.

McClella, Randall. *The Healing Forces of Music*. Amity House, Inc., Amity, New York, 1988.

McLeod, Norma, and Marcia Herndon. *The Ethnography of Musical Performance*. Darby: Norwood Editions, 1980.

Mensah, Augustine N. *The Black Aesthetic: A Cross-Cultural Perspective*. Ann Arbor, MI: University Microfilms, 1979.

Merriam, Alan P. *The Anthropology of Music*. Evanston: Northwestern University Press, 1964.

Merriam-Webster. *A.Webster's New Collegiate Dictionary*, 8th ed., 1973.

Mondet, Bernard and Adama Drame Jacket Notes. *Rhythms of the Manding-Adama Drame (Jembe)*. Unesco Collection, Musical Sources, The Language of Rhythm III-3. London: Philips 6586 042 (LP disc), 1979.

Nketia, J. H. Kwabena. *Drumming in Akan Communities of Ghana*. London: University of Ghana and Thomas Nelson and Sons, Ltd., 1963.

_____. "Tradition and Innovation in African Music," *Jamaica Journal, Quarterly of the Institute of Jamaica*, 2, 3-4 (1968): 2-9.

_____. *The Music of Africa*. New York: W. W. Norton & Company, 1974.

_____. "The Aesthetic Dimensions in Ethnomusicological Studies," *World of Music* 26, 1 (1984): 3-28.

_____. "Processes of Differentiation and Interdependency in African Music: The Case of Asante and Her Neighbors," *Journal of the International Institute for Comparative Music Studies and Documentation* (Berlin) in Association with the International Music Council (UNESCO) 28, 2 (1986a): 41-55.

Olatunji, Babatunde. "Invocation of the Orisas (The GODS KORI, OGUN, and SHANGO)," Los Angeles Theater Center, Program Notes of 27 April, 1986.

Padgette, Paul. *The Dance Photography of Carl Van Vechten*. New York: Macmillan Publishing Co., Inc., 1981.

Pantaleoni, Hewitt. "Toward Understanding the Play of Sogo in Atsia," *Ethnomusicology* 16, 1 (1972): 1-37.

Pennington, Dorothy L. "Time in African Culture," in *African Culture: The Rhythms of Unity*, Edited by Molefe Kete Asante and Kariamu Welsh Asante. Trenton: African World Press, Inc. (1990), 123-140.

Piston, Walter. *Harmony*. New York: W. W. Norton & Company, Inc., 1987.

Pwono, Mondondo. "The Relevance of Traditional Elements in African Contemporary Music in Zaire," *Pan Africanism and Conflict Resolution*. Terre Haute: Indiana State University Press, 1988.

Qureshi, Regula Burkhardt. "Musical Sound and Contextual Input: A Performance Model for Musical Analysis," *Ethnomusicology* 31 (Winter, 1987): 56-86.

Rex, Chris. *Comfort Clothes*. Millbrae, Ca.: Celestial Arts, 1981.

Roberts, John Storm. *Black Music of Two Worlds*. New York: Praeger Publication Inc., 1972

Rouget, Gilbert. *Music and Trance*. Chicago: University of Chicago Press., 1985.

Seeger, Charles. "Systematic Musicology: Viewpoints, Orientations and Methods," *Journal of the American Musicological Society* 4 (1951): 240-248.

Sidran, Ben. *Black Talk*. New York: Holt, Rinehart and Winston, 1971.

Simmons, William S. *Eyes of the Night, Witchcraft Among a Sénégalese People*. Boston: Little Brown and Company, Inc., 1971.

Simpson, George Eaton. *Religious Cults of the Caribbean: Trinidad, Jamaica and Haiti*. Puerto Rico: University of Puerto Rico, 1980.

Southern, Eileen. *The Music of Black Americans, a History*. New York: W. W. Norton & Company, 1983.

Spencer, Paul. *Society and the Dance*. London: Cambridge University Press, 1985.

Stearns, Marshall W. *The Story of Jazz*. New York: Oxford University Press, 1956.

Stearns, Marshall and Jean Stearns. *Jazz Dance*. New York: Macmillan Company, 1968.

Staats, Florence Joan. *Toward a Black Aesthetic in The Visual Arts*. Ann Arbor, MI: University Microfilms, 1978

Tracey, Hugh. *CHOPI MUSICIANS, Their Music, Poetry and Instruments*. London: Oxford University Press, 1970.

Tucker, Iantha Elizabeth Lake. *The Role of Afro-Americans in Dance in the United States from Slavery Through 1983: A Slide Presentation*. Ann Arbor, MI: University Microfilms, 1984.

Van Sertima, Ivan. *They Came Before Columbus*. New York: Random House, 1970.

Van Vechten, Carl. *The Dance Photography of Carl Van Vechten*. New York: Shirmer Books, 1981.

Ventura, Michael. *Shadow Dancing in the USA*. Los Angeles: Jeremy P. Tarcher, Inc., 1985.

Washington, Ernest L., M.D. "The Talking Drum!" *The Black Dance Newsletter* 1, 1 (May, 1989):19-20.

Welsh Asante, Kariamu. "The Jerusarema Dance and Zimbabwe." *Journal of Black Studies* 15, 4 (1985): 181-403.

_____. "Commonalities in African Dance: An Aesthetic Foundation," in *African Culture: The Rhythms of Unity.* Edited by Molefe Kete Asante and Kariamu Welsh-Asante. Trenton: African World Press, Inc. (1990), 71-82.

Wilson, Olly. "The Association of Movement and Music as a Manifestation of a 1981 Black Conceptual Approach to Music-Making," in *More Than Dancing—Essays on Afro-American Music and Musicians.* Edited by Irene V. Jackson. Westport: Greenwood Press (1985), 9-24.

Witsen, Leo Van. *Costuming for Opera.* Bloomington: Indiana University Press, 1981.

Wright, Donald R. "Oral Tradition from the Gambia: Mandinka Griots," *Papers On International Studies* Vol. 1, No. 37. Athens, Ohio: Center for International Studies, 1979.

Zirimu, Pio and Andrew Gurr, ed. *Black Aesthetics: Papers from a Colloquium Held at the University of Nairobi, June 1971.* Nairobi: East African Literature Bureau, 1973.

Index

Also available from White Cliffs!
The Performance in World Music Series

✓ *Mandiani Drum and Dance: Djimbe Performance and Black Aesthetics from Africa to the New World*. Mark Sunkett. Book, $19.95. Performance CD of Mandiani and other genres recorded in Sénégal, $15.95. Aural Examples cassette, $12.95. Instructional video, $79.95 libraries, $39.95 individuals.

✓ *The Drums of Vodou*. Lois Wilcken featuring Frisner Augustin. Book, $19.95. Compact disc featuring Frisner Augustin, $15.95.

✓ *The Music of Santería: Traditional Rhythms of the Batá Drums*. John Amira and Steven Cornelius. Book, $19.95. Compact disc, $15.95.

✓ *Drum Gahu: The Rhythms of West African Drumming*. David Locke. Book, $19.95. Performance of Gahu recorded in Africa on compact disc, $15.95. Aural Examples cassette, $12.95.

✓ *Kpegisu: A War Drum of the Ewe*. David Locke. Book, $19.95. Aural Examples cassette, $12.95. Video Documentary Performance. VHS video filmed in Africa by master musician Godwin Agbeli, $79.95 libraries, $39.95 individuals. Kpegisu: Video Master Class. Godwin Agbeli performs sequences of Kpegisu, keyed to examples from the book, $59.95 libraries, $34.95 individuals.

✓ *Drum Damba: Talking Drum Lessons*. David Locke featuring Abubakari Lunna. Book, $19.95. Aural Examples cassette, $12.95.

✓ *Salsa!: The Rhythm of Latin Music*. Charley Gerard with Marty Sheller. Book, $17.95. Aural Examples cassette, $12.95.

✓ *Xylophone Music from Ghana*. Trevor Wiggins and Joseph Kobom. Book, $15.95. Performances by Joseph Kobom on compact disc, $15.95.

Orders: **WHITE CLIFFS MEDIA**
c/o Pathway Book Service
4 White Brook Rd, Gilsum, NH 03448   1.800.345.6665
www.whitecliffsmedia.com